An Angel,
a Book,
and a Secret

~~~~~~~~~~~

Memoir

Pauline Pilote Eby

SONG OF THE GARDEN PUBLISHING

Song of the Garden Publishing
piloteeby@gmail.com

Cover design by Angela Eisenbart

Printed in the United States of America

ISBN Paperback: 979-8-9887815-0-9
ISBN eBook: 979-8-9887815-1-6

Excerpts from "The Fourth CARP Convention" by Claus Dubisz reprinted by permission.

For God speaks in one way,
and in two, though man does not perceive it.
In a dream, in a vision of the night,
when deep sleep falls upon men,
while they slumber on their beds,
then he opens the ears of men....

—Job 33:14-16

Contents

Voices in the Night

It all started with the dream that wasn't a dream. For ten years, the essence of that night vision subconsciously pulled me forward. Like an app running in the background, a mysterious *something* was pointing me in the direction of finding and unlocking a secret. I had no idea that I was on a journey, let alone where that journey would take me.

Prior to the dream was a traumatic event that began on a warm day in July when my father stayed home from work. As he lay on the sofa, he turned to our neighbor and said, "Pauline doesn't care that I'm sick."

I was mortified. It was far from true, but in keeping with the norms of our family culture, I said nothing. I was twelve years old.

Mrs. Cote responded on my behalf. "Oh yes, she does. She's worried. She says you never stay home, even when you're sick. She's afraid there must be something wrong."

He smiled.

Later that evening he asked me, "May I borrow your blanket tonight?" He was referring to my lightweight cotton blanket.

He had decided to sleep on the sofa, partly to be propped up there and partly because the cool night air from the living room windows would be soothing. But it might get chilly, so he wanted a blanket.

It was odd of him to ask this of me. He could easily have asked my mother to bring him a blanket. Instead, he asked me. And he asked for *that* blanket. Did he know it was my favorite?

It was new, a blanket just for me, just for my bed. It was beautiful, with a colorful pattern of bold stripes in a lightweight cotton weave, perfect for summer evenings. I cherished that blanket. Did he know?

It became my offering. I was happy to do *something* for him, to show that I did, in fact, care. I covered him with my blanket.

Later, in the middle of the night, I awoke to the sound of his desperate voice calling for my mother. "Jean! Jean!"

From my room upstairs, I sensed his urgency. "Mom! Mom! Dad's calling you!" I cried out into the night.

My mother's bare feet padded toward the living room. I held my breath, straining to listen, to hear their voices and know that everything was fine. Fear gripped me. I couldn't move. Time stopped and reality was strangely bent and warped.

"Please don't let Daddy die," I begged God. "If you let him live, I'll say the rosary every day for as long as I live. I promise!"

I stopped in my tracks. *How dare I bargain with the Almighty?* I was a mere created being, according to my Catholic upbringing, and here I was … crossing an uncrossable boundary. I repented. I promised God that *regardless* of the outcome, *whatever* His will, I would henceforth pray the rosary every day, for no other reason than because it was the right thing to do.

Thus immersed in my petitions, I was oblivious to what had been happening downstairs. How much time had elapsed? It was still dark outside, but now there were voices that were not those of my parents. Once again, I was terrified. I would not go down there to have the dreadful truth confirmed.

New voices continued to drift up to my room. Grandparents, aunts, and uncles arrived to comfort my mother and help care for the five semi-orphaned children. They spoke quietly. From time to time I heard my mother sob, "What am I going to do? I'm pregnant." A sixth child on the way was news to me.

In a willful paralysis, barely breathing, I continued to lie in bed. As long as I could endure my self-imposed exile, I could still *hope*. But soon it was long past time to get up. My younger sister, with whom I shared the room, began to stir. She sat up, breaking my trance. Her rising would open the floodgates to an unstoppable river of reality. "Jackie!" I whispered, "Don't go down there!"

She looked at me, rose, and walked down the stairs.

Eventually I, too, had to get up. Although I joined the world of the living, I kept aloof, ignoring them as though they were invisible. On their part, they observed me in silence, except for the few who whispered, "She knows."

I stood there, looking at my weeping mother, her own mother at her side. My four siblings, ranging in age from two to ten, were in the room. Sobbing, sitting, or standing in a room full of adults, each orphaned child seemed alone and un-consoled. Each hovered in his or her own orbit circling the mother, a sun that no longer shone.

At the wake and at the funeral, I avoided looking at the body. It was a classic case of denial. As long as there was no body, I could keep death at a distance. I could cling to the illusion that he was still alive.

My wishful thinking was abetted by the Cold War, which in 1964 was threatening to escalate. Even as a twelve-year-old, I was aware of some of the issues. *My father is a respected police officer, a hero,* I thought. *He isn't dead at all. The CIA has recruited him. They came in the middle of the night, in secret, and whisked him away to serve his country. He's in the USSR now, working as a spy. He'll be fine; I'll see him again someday.* Such was the desperate reasoning of a child.

Nevertheless, somewhere in the murky hours or days that followed his death, I had a moment of clarity in which I became aware that from now on I would have to take care of myself. I would have to find my own way. My father had been our guiding light and now he was gone.

The lightweight cotton blanket with the lovely bold stripes made its way back onto my bed. The mantle that had covered my father would now cover me.

The Dream

And it shall come to pass ...
That I will pour out my spirit on all flesh;
Your sons and your daughters shall prophesy,
Your old men shall dream dreams,
And your young men shall see visions.
                                    —Joel 2: 28-29

A nd so it came to pass that sometime later, within a year of this event, I had the dream that was not a dream.

I left my body, guided by an angel. Fully aware that my body was lying in bed, I traveled with the angel to a place ... somewhere deep in the cosmos.

There the angel informed me of something of cosmic significance, critical information about human history and the present era. It had to do with the new wine that Jesus had promised, the many things he had yet to tell us but which we were "not yet ready" to hear.[1]

---

[1] *John* 16 :12

The angel placed a book in my hands. It contained the details, the heart and soul of the new wine. Together we turned the pages and conversed. In some fashion, I absorbed the contents of the book.

Although young, I realized the significance of the information and assured the angel of my intention to help. Excitedly I proclaimed to him my plan. "People don't know this! When I wake up, I'll tell them. I'll tell everyone! They need to know!"

The angel was solemn. His response was grave. "I'm sorry," he said, "but when you awaken, you will not remember any of this. Not until the time is right."

I was incredulous. This was too important to forget. I clenched my fists and called out my resolve. "No! I *have to* remember! I *will* remember!"

I strained with all my might and all my will to hold on to that revelation. I rehearsed it over and over to keep it fresh and vivid in my mind, so it would resound like a mantra when I awoke.

But it was no use.

I awoke in my bed, sobbing and passionately repeating, "I have to remember! It's too important. I *have to* remember!"

But I couldn't. I couldn't recall a thing. Not the angel, not the subject matter, not a clue. All I knew was that I had dreamed something important and that it was essential that I recall what it was. I sat up, wracking my brain, trying with all my might to remember as the tears poured down my cheeks. *If only I can catch a glimmer! Just a hint!*

But it was useless. As the angel had promised, I would remember … only at the appointed time.

Growing up in Maine

I asked my mother recently, "Do you remember when I was young … I was crying so hard because I couldn't remember a dream?"

"No."

"Do you remember *anything* unusual about me?"

"Well, you stayed in your room reading all the time."

My siblings agree: "All you ever did was read."

The truth is that from that day forward I was on fire to read. For reasons unknown to me, I determined that I would read every book ever published. Because I was so young, the impossibility of achieving such a task did not occur to me.

Other than this, I was a normal child growing up in Lewiston, Maine. Some of my fondest memories are embedded in Maine's natural beauty. Her clean air, forests, mountains, lakes, and shorelines are etched into my sensory memory. Family gatherings and outings, and even my father's choice of a house on a hilltop meant that we were surrounded by Maine's awe-inspiring scenery. A simple meal on the backyard picnic table entailed being embraced by a green yard dotted with boulders (remnants of melted glaciers), fruit trees, and a forest of birch and pine that stretched on and on down a gently sloping hill.

Among the sensations I recall, only one was less than delightful. It was the smell of the Androscoggin River on a foggy day. Back then, the river was polluted with industrial waste, especially from the lumber, paper, and pulp industries that were upriver. The smell was powerful. Carried on the fog, it wafted for miles, all the way to the top of the hill on which our house sat.

Other than that occasional stench, my memories of Maine are blissful. At the Sunday River ski resort, my siblings, aunts, and I stand atop one of the mountains adjusting our gear. Along with the fresh cold air, we inhale awesome panoramas of sunny blue skies, glittering snow, and the forested peaks of the Mahoosuc Range, a northerly extension of the White Mountains.

In another winter memory, my siblings and I are ice fishing with our dad. The frozen lake, snugly invisible beneath a white blanket, is silent. Forest surrounds. Atop the lake rests our ice shanty, inside of which burns the compact wood stove that warms us when we come inside, exhausted from skating on the rink that we've shoveled clear of snow.

Then there's summer, and a narrow road winds down toward the ocean at Small Point. The pavement narrows and dissolves to dirt and pebble, coming to rest at a sandy beach, a lagoon, and the cliffs upon which vacationers from across the ocean camp.

We lived on a dirt road on the outskirts of town. From time to time, the Public Works Department would spray a thin oily film on the surface of the road to keep the dust down. Regardless, between sprayings, with every passing car dense clouds of dust would rise from the ground, dissipating only ever so slowly. There's a saying that country folk watch the grass grow. Well, one of *our* pastimes was to watch the dust settle.

Old Greene Road was about as far from the river as one could get. Surrounded by dense woods, our house sat securely atop the highest hill in Lewiston. My father had selected this spot to ensure that we would never have to experience, as he had, the often-seasonal flooding of the Androscoggin River.

Dad was born and raised in his family's ancestral home on River Road. Although the house stood on an elevated bank a good thirty feet from the river's edge, thanks to cold winters, thick ice, and the heavy snowfall of southeastern Maine, it was not unusual for the Androscoggin to overflow its banks and flood their home during spring thaws. Besides the flooding, there were the river rats to contend with. I once watched my grandmother use a broom to bravely shoo one off her porch.

Considering what life along the river meant, it must have been stressful for my father, as a child, to live under those circumstances. Although several generations of his family had lived there, he chose to locate his own growing family in a place of safety, far from unruly waters, atop that high hill. Our home had the added virtue of being only minutes away from a Catholic elementary school.

Raffles

We had a German Shepherd named Raffles. Although I can't be certain, he may have been a retired police dog. Whatever his origin, Dad had volunteered to give him a home and we fell in love with him. From all appearances, he loved us back.

Together with the dog, Dad often visited his mother, our Mémère, down on River Road. On one of those visits Raffles, who had a habit of chasing cars, got hit by one. He ran off, dazed, to lick his wounds … or to die.

My father went after him, calling and searching, but Raffles was nowhere to be found. Dad returned home without him. We were heartbroken.

Over the next several weeks, Dad would often stop by his mother's house to scour the neighborhood and ask about the dog. No one had seen him. Then one day the entire family headed out to visit Mémère. We took the usual route down the steep hill of South Avenue, over the railroad tracks and toward the river and River Road.

I had never lost hope of finding Raffles. Whenever we approached that vicinity, I would scan the horizon, hoping to see him. Today was no different. As we drove down the hill, I sat up in the back seat and craned my neck, straining to see along the length of track that ran behind the houses. This time, in the distance, I spotted the silhouette of a dog.

"It's Raffles!" I cried out. "Stop the car!"

Dad crossed the tracks and jerked the car to a stop. The doors flew open and everyone jumped out. Could it be? Was it really Raffles?

I ran along the tracks and called at the top of my lungs, "Raffles! Raffles!" The dog raised his head in recognition. He bolted toward us. He was a race horse, head down, neck outstretched and running with all his might along that length of track. He jumped into our waiting arms, knocking us over, fiercely wagging his tail and entire body. He was ecstatic, all wags and tongue, yelping and whining uncontrollably as he licked our faces over and over again. I hugged him tight and burrowed into his fur.

Little Sister

My relationship with my younger sister was sometimes strained. It was plagued by sibling rivalry.

One afternoon, when I was about six and she was four, the school bus dropped me off in front of the house. Jackie was there, sitting on the front steps as usual, waiting for me. She was quietly absorbed, playing with something. As I looked more closely, I saw that it was a tiny box containing a double-edged razor blade.

This was *not* a normal part of our afternoon routine. I looked around for my mother but didn't see her.

"Where did you get that?" I asked Jackie.

"Mom said I could have it," she replied.

I shrugged. *If it's okay with Mom, then it's not my business.* I went inside and began my after-school routine of snack and homework.

A short while later, I heard my mother scream. Then, from my room upstairs, I heard their faint voices, Mom's and my sister's, out there on the porch. Mom was upset. *Jackie's in trouble*, I thought.

In the very next moment, my mother bellowed, "Pauline! Come down here! Now!"

I jumped up and ran to them. There on the porch sat Jackie, looking sweet and innocent. I turned to my mother. "What?"

She glared at me and roared "Why did you give her a razor blade?"

Jackie watched calmly as I proclaimed my innocence. On my part, the protest was a mere formality. After a few years of being my sister's scapegoat, I had learned that to object was a vain endeavor.

My mother ran out of ways of scolding me. She wrapped it up with "Go to your room! No supper for you!"

And that was that.

Later, from upstairs in my room, I could hear the family dinner in progress. Though I couldn't make out the conversation, I assumed that my father was receiving the report of my alleged bad behavior. Because of his wisdom and police experience, he cross-examined the prosecutor and her main witness. In the end, the witness confessed to having committed the crime herself. She had taken the razor blade from the medicine cabinet. I was exonerated. Case dismissed.

From the kitchen, my mother's voice called up, "Pauline! You can come down now." I was allowed to eat supper. But I hungered more for an apology that never came.

Based on this episode, it won't surprise the reader to learn that I had conflicting feelings about my little sister. From time to time those feelings surfaced and I had to grapple with them.

There was that one memorable day at Small Point beach. I was still not much older than six or seven. I sat on a blanket, enjoying the warmth of the midday sun. My eyes embraced the soft, swaying pine trees that bordered the lagoon. An ocean breeze played gently over the still, sparkling water.

Jackie, the little cherub, the apple of my father's eye, waded along the shore, watching tiny fish dart to and fro at her feet. Because this tableau disturbed my peaceful meditation, I looked away. I tried to recapture the soothing solitude of the warm embracing stillness that melded and meshed with the quiet voices of my aunts who sat nearby, out of view but pleasantly audible.

Then, once again, the stillness was disturbed. This time the water moved and rippled where, a moment ago, Jackie had been wading. Then a head bobbed up.

The quiet conversations continued, the silence of the lagoon lingered, but little sister was silent as she bobbed up and down gasping for air. She had stepped into a hole lurking in the water.

Her little feet touched bottom. Her toes pushed, shoved, and propelled her little cherub's body back up to the surface, up to the air that she gulped before sinking back down into the pit.

In one heartbeat, a solution to the sibling rivalry that had plagued me flashed before my eyes. But even as a child, I must have realized that her death was not an appropriate solution. With the next beat of my heart, my voice shattered the calm. "Jackie's drowning!"

I stood and pointed. My cousin and her friend leapt from their perch on a raft. They splashed through the shallows to snatch up the child and carry her to shore. They swaddled the little cherub in a clean towel.

And all was calm again as peace returned to my world.

Roots

My family is French-Canadian in origin. Our great-grandparents emigrated from Quebec Province in the late nineteenth century, when the booming factories of the Industrial Revolution attracted almost a million French Canadians to jobs in Maine.

Back then, the Anglo-French antipathies of the colonial period lingered. French-Catholic immigrants faced intense opposition from English Protestants who had settled New England before them. Even as late as 1919, laws were passed outlawing the use of the French language. Throughout the 1920s, the Ku Klux Klan actively targeted the French-speaking population, the Catholic Church, and the Jewish population in Maine. By 1925, twenty-three percent of Maine's residents were members of the KKK. [2]

I was unaware of this history until recently. My family was proud of its French-Catholic culture. In fact, we

---

[2] Nadeau, "KKK contre les Français du Maine."

continued speaking French until the day Daddy laid down the law that all of us, grandparents included, would from that day forward speak only English at home.

I have reflected upon possible reasons for his strong feelings on the subject. I suspect that, when the anti-French-language laws were repealed in 1960, my father may have feared that a return to French immersion might isolate his children from opportunities that came with fluency in English. He wanted us to fit in with the broader culture and the economy of the more established English-Protestant population.

A black-and-white photograph of my father's parents sits on a shelf in my living room. It's a formal portrait: a suit and tie for my grandfather, a dark dress and a string of pearls for my grandmother.

William Henri is a handsome man with wavy brown conservatively cut hair that sits atop a high forehead above an angular face. His story is legendary. Our elders say that he played vaudeville. That makes sense because he was born, not in the Maine woods, but in Potsdam, New York. He was a violinist. Or perhaps he considered himself a fiddler. Did he play classical music or the French jigs and country music that were popular back then?

Sadly, I never heard him play. Before I was born, his arm was shot off in a hunting accident near his home along the Androscoggin. That marked the end of his fiddling career

… although one of my sisters distinctly remembers him playing with his one arm.

I recall Pépère's half-arm, the stump where his arm should have been. Most of the time it was encased in a shirt sleeve neatly folded up and tucked in. But I never felt that he was handicapped. I never saw him unable to do anything, including tie his own shoelaces. In fact, he taught me to tie *my* shoes.

I remember the cool, dimly lit living room in the house on River Road. I can still see my grandfather sitting in his chair, bent over, chin resting on his knees, slowly tying and untying his own shoelaces. He speaks softly as he demonstrates first how to make one loop, then another, and then join the two into a perfect knot.

It seemed so complicated back then, and yet without fail he was able to do it each time. I sat on the carpet at his feet, watching intently. With my tiny fingers, I imitated his actions, but without success. "Do it again!" I begged for the tenth time.

Patiently he would repeat the process, using his one hand. I strained to make the loops on my own shoelaces and then tie them together in a bow, just as he had. We labored together in that peaceful stillness. The only sound in the room, other than our soft voices, came from my steady breathing and the ticking of the clock.

Finally, I squealed with delight. "I did it! I did it!"

"*Bien! Voila!* You did it! *Mémère, viens ici!* Pauline can tie her shoes."

My grandmother ran into the room and beamed in admiration as I proudly demonstrated my new skill.

That was my grandmother Éliane.[3] In the portrait on the shelf in my living room, she stands beside her husband and looks out at the world with intelligent eyes and a noble brow. One eye seems larger. In photos of spiritually attuned people, I have noticed that their eyes don't match. One eye seems exacting, piercing, or keenly observant, while the other is gentle and kind. One eye looks through you, while the other seems to love you unconditionally.

Éliane's eyebrows are symmetrical. She wears no makeup. Even as a young woman, she dressed simply and in good taste. She was regal, poised, calm. In the photo, her mouth has only the barest trace of a smile. I don't ever recall her joking or horsing around.

I wonder whether her life with William Henri was challenging. He was a musician; artists can be temperamental, avant-garde, and nonconformist. She was a pious Roman Catholic and sixteen years his junior.

Éliane's family was supportive. The Chamberlains were compassionate, charitable folk. They ran a grocery store and, according to family legend, during the Great Depression provided food to customers *on credit* in the days before credit

---

[3] It intrigues me that, although we were French, the name *Éliane* in Hebrew means "my God has answered."

cards existed, knowing that they'd probably never see the money. Their house and home overflowed with people and with love.

Éliane grew up in that house. She birthed her own children there. Years later, she and Henri welcomed their youngest son—my father—and his pregnant wife and two children to come live with them.

The house itself sat not far from the edge of the south bank of the Androscoggin, just outside the neighborhood called "Little Canada." There were those floods and river rats to contend with. And then, of course, there was the loss of Henri's arm.

Éliane's faith must have sustained her. She prayed daily and attended Mass and received the sacraments more often than the Catholic faith officially required. Books on the lives of saints graced the shelves of her library. As a child, I immersed myself in those books and meditated on the remarkable lives of those men and women.

Éliane's piety rubbed off on me. I developed a life of prayer. I thought about God, Jesus, and the plight of humanity. For me, those were essential realities.

On my mother's side are the Poulins and the Gonthiers. A wedding photo of my mother's parents, Jeannette and Arthur, displays a large bouquet of roses, a satiny dress, a perfectly crimped hairdo, and a suit and tie. Jeannette's nervous disposition is visible. Arthur, standing beside her, seems severe.

As children, we took for granted the generosity of these grandparents. Their income was hardly adequate, yet every Friday evening they provided a feast to please the hearts and ease the hunger of their six semi-orphaned grandchildren. They brought to our table a plentiful mix of KFC fare, spaghetti and Italian sandwiches from Luigi's, or McDonalds burgers and fries. Food was love. It fed the bodies and went a long way toward healing the souls of the fatherless children who, for the rest of the week, lived on government surplus American cheese, powdered milk, and whatever else the welfare check could provide.

My mother's parents and grandparents had few material assets. There was virtually nothing to show for their lifelong labors in the mills and factories. A tiny wooden house on factory-owned land was all they had. The land itself was sometimes drowned in spring thaws when the river brimmed and overflowed from the melting snow and ice. That humble house, which had once belonged to Arthur's parents, was their greatest material achievement.

After their children had grown, Jeannette and Arthur moved back into that house where Arthur's aged mother, my great-grandmother Rosalie, was still living. I remember her sitting at a small table in the tiny kitchen that could barely hold that table and its four chairs, a tiny sink, a stove, a refrigerator and, in the corner, a simple rocker by a lone window. Later, I remember her as she lay in a small bed in the adjoining room, the tiny living room-turned-sickroom, from where she departed the world.

They had so little.

Day in and day out, my grandparents and their parents before them worked long hard hours at factory and mill jobs for minimal wages, most often paid by the piece (*piece work*, it was called). They bent their heads over industrial sewing machines, stitching shoe leather. They breathed glue and other noxious fumes. Or they worked at the looms, weaving cloth.

In the dim light, they strained their eyes and bent their necks in airless factories with worn wooden staircases, rickety wooden elevators, and broken windows that were either stuck or bolted shut. I know this because I, too, worked in one of those factories, alongside my grandmother, during summer breaks from school.

Knowing all of this, knowing the burden of the monotonous, arduous labor that bore so little fruit, I can appreciate the significance of the sacrifice and expense that were lavished upon Jeannette's wedding, her "special day" as documented in the photo on my shelf. The hairstyle alone represents a substantial investment. That was not my grandmother's usual style. On that day, every lock was in place, expertly and tightly coifed. And the extravagant bouquet shouts of a proud refusal to be perceived as being poor, lower class, or inferior. Of all the wedding photos I've seen, from any era, no bouquet seems quite so grand.

Although the two sides of my family, maternal and paternal, were from slightly different economic and educational strata, the public schools, mills, and factories tossed people together and mixed the disparate groups. In fact, a factory, the Federal Shoe Company, was where my parents met.

Gifts from Catholicism

The piety of my grandmother Éliane and the teachings and traditions of the Catholic Church planted within me the seeds of a spirituality that sprouted, took root, and grew. I benefited greatly from my Catholic upbringing, and for that I'm thankful.

Growing up, I was surrounded by the saints and traditions of Catholicism. From a young age, I began to pray, thinking about God and Jesus. As I sat in church inhaling the incense, gazing at the statues, and listening to the priests chant the Latin Mass as they went through the motions that were to transform bread and wine into the body and blood of Christ, I pondered the theological concepts.[4]

---

[4] Catholic children begin to receive education in dogmatic or theological concepts at the age of six or seven. That is because they are expected to partake in the sacrament of Holy Communion, for the first time, at the age of seven, which is considered to be the "age of reason."

The parochial school I attended provided a protective and embracing environment. The nuns were devoted to their profession of educating and nurturing young souls. In addition to its spiritual benefits, Holy Family School offered an excellent academic foundation.

Back then, a Catholic education was free for children of "practicing" Catholics, meaning those who regularly attended Mass, observed the Holy Days of Obligation, and tithed. That's because in those days it was the men and women of the religious orders, the priests and nuns, who served as teachers. They required no salaries or benefits, so the cost of running a school was far less than it is today.

Later, when membership in the religious orders dwindled and schools had to hire the laity as teachers, the payment of salaries and benefits radically increased the cost of education. Only then did Catholic schools begin to charge tuition.

Thus, my siblings and I were blessed with a quality private school education at no cost. That situation became precarious, however, when our father died at the age of thirty-five. An officer of the Lewiston Police Department for almost ten years, he died just a few weeks short of qualifying to receive a pension. The family became destitute. We had to rely on government welfare. As a result, we were no longer able to contribute the expected tithes to the church. My mother and grandparents worried that this might mean the end of Catholic schooling for us.

Somehow, the church parish came through with a solution that may have been influenced by the respect the community had for my father. The family, including the children, would tithe in the form of volunteering their time to the church and the school.

I was only vaguely aware of this arrangement. I did notice that, in the school year following my father's death, the nuns were especially solicitous and compassionate. They took me under their wings. They assigned me small tasks and responsibilities, both at school and in the church building located next door.

In the classrooms, I helped sweep and polish the wooden floors. We used a pinkish material, something like shredded rubber erasers, sprinkled over the floor. We spread and rubbed this around with rags that we stepped on and dragged under our feet. It was like ice skating … more fun than work. I also cleaned chalkboards and hung out of open windows smacking erasers together to remove the chalk dust. That was fun, too.

I enjoyed spending time with the kind, loving nuns like Sister Mary Edwards and Sister Saint Lucille. And it was fun because sometimes other students, perhaps some who had been assigned to detention, were also part of the activities.

More than anything, I loved to clean the church. Holy Family Church was a large modern structure of polished marble, stained-glass windows, and huge wooden doors. From my youthful perspective, looking out the classroom window and across the parking lot, the church seemed like a cathedral.

I loved the church on those afternoons at recess time. While other students played noisily in the schoolyard, the silence inside the church was holy. There was a peace that was almost tangible, and it seemed as though one's thoughts and prayers went straight to God. The sanctuary was cool and dim. Light filtered in through the transparent, brightly-colored saints who stood or knelt in prayer and adoration.

I helped Sister Saint Lucille clean this holy space. For the most part, we worked in prayerful silence, but sometimes she took the time to talk quietly or to explain things. She spoke with me respectfully, as though I was worthy of her time and attention.

With a soft dust mop, I mopped and shone the vast marble floor of the sanctuary. I dusted the pews and replaced votive candles in the small shrines or alcoves that dotted the church's inner perimeter. If I finished my tasks early, I'd climb the steps to the altar and walk behind it into the sacristy, the preparation area for the priests. I watched as Sister Saint Lucille, with heart and hands of devotion, cleaned the sacred vessels for the wine and the Eucharist. I watched her set out the holy vestments for the priest to wear.

The holiness of the sanctuary was palpable. Cleaning the church was a sacred experience for me. Thanks to this privileged assignment, I had occasion to pray and worship in the quiet church, alone. I remember one prayer at a Station of the Cross. Meditating on the heartbreaking agony of Jesus, I wept as I tried to comfort him.

On another occasion, during Mass, I was shaken by an unexpected apprehension. The congregation was reciting the *Nicene Creed*. When we came to the part about the return of Christ, "I believe … he will come again in glory to judge the living and the dead," I stopped in my tracks. For some reason, the possibility seemed real and imminent. I fervently begged, *Please God! If this happens in my lifetime, please don't let me miss it!*

From where did such a passionate concern arise? If Christ were coming on the clouds, then surely no one would miss him.

Was it possible that he might come in a different way … more like a thief in the night? In that case, he would hardly be noticed, at least not at first.

What if he is born again, on the earth? Is it possible that, as they did two thousand years ago, people might fail to recognize him as the Christ?

Why was I so worried about the possibility of missing the second coming? In hindsight now, I see that the recitation of the Creed at that moment triggered something in my subconscious mind. It had to do with that angel in my dream and his explanation about the second coming.

Quest

Although I had forgotten the dream, I believe my obsession with reading was connected to the book the angel had placed in my hands. My subconscious mind—or whatever force was moving me forward on that quest—surely knew that the book held the key to what the angel had revealed. All I had to do was find it.

I believe that's why, even as a child, I kept to myself and read. I was obsessed with an unquenchable thirst for knowledge. I read avidly, first everything in my own house and then from my cousin's library. Later, as a teen, I opened an account at the Lewiston Public Library. I walked there every Friday after school, returning one pile of books and checking out another.

At first I enjoyed science fiction, including the stories of Ray Bradbury. Then I gravitated toward reports about purported experiences with aliens and UFOs. I was especially impressed by accounts that testified to aliens as benevolent, more advanced beings who came to help humanity out of its morass of ignorance, cruelty, and suffering. I yearned to join them to heal humanity of its brokenness and to create an enlightened, peaceful world.

Gradually my reading progressed to a more focused search for wisdom and truth. But what was I looking for?

I read biographies and other nonfiction, books about ancient Egypt and Greece, about Marxism, communism, the history of Southeast Asia. On my grandmother's shelf, I discovered Tom Dooley and Albert Schweitzer; they became my role models. I decided that I would become a doctor. I would heal the powerless and the destitute as these noble men had done. Somewhere along the way, I also decided that I would learn Russian so that I could contribute to peaceful dialogue with our Cold War enemies.[5]

---

[5] Later, when I went to college, I still had these goals. I became a pre-med biology major and studied Russian.

People of God

As my quest for truth evolved, I found myself in search of a new community of faith, one that was more closely aligned with my ideas regarding a holy community or, as I conceived of it, a *people of God*. The germ of this idea had been planted earlier, at the time of my childhood dream of the angel. It had lain dormant in my subconscious mind until it was triggered to sprout, one sunny Sunday morning after Mass.

I noticed that, instead of lingering to chat and find ways to "love thy neighbor," the parishioners were in a great hurry to leave church. Whole families were rushing out and piling into cars to get away. The parking lot was crowded and every driver seemed angry or impatient. Each one was cussing the other, making angry gestures and honking his horn. Even my father joined the chorus.

The scene startled me. It imprinted itself upon my mind as being the opposite of brotherly love. It provided such a stark contrast to the holiness of those same people who, just a few moments earlier, had been sitting in church, heads piously bowed, hands folded in prayer.

Although the incident bothered me, I stored it away together with other things that I later found puzzling. For example, questions were triggered by elements in my Catholic education, beginning in elementary school and continuing on through public high school as I attended weekly C.C.D. (Confraternity of Christian Doctrine) classes with fellow Catholic youth.

As a good Catholic, I had learned to respect the priests and nuns as representatives of God and Christ. We had been taught that these men and women were of a higher calling and that they were worthy shepherds of the people. To my trusting mind, their word—as well as that of the Pope—was not to be questioned.

That blind faith began to unravel, however, after one C.C.D. class. I was trying to understand a point of doctrine that seemed contrary to fact. It didn't make sense to me, so I raised my hand. "How can that be? Can you explain?"

Instead of clarifying or even attempting to clarify, Sister Saint Agnes looked at me and paused. She folded her hands as though in prayer, but her face and body had turned to stone. "That ... is ... a ... Mystery," she said slowly and deliberately. She rocked back on the heels of her black pumps, then touched down again. "It cannot be explained," the nun continued. "You must accept it on faith." Then she stood motionless, anchored to the floor. In her mind, the problem had been solved.

Everyone was silent. There were no further questions. No one dared.

But I was not satisfied. Regardless of God's awesomeness, omnipotence, and all the rest, I felt that God had given me a mind for comprehension—of Himself as well as the universe. Because of that, to propose doctrine that was contrary to reason or that could not even *begin* to be explained was inadequate.

That experience placed a thorn in my side. But it was not the decisive moment that propelled me away from the "One True Faith." That came later.

For many Catholics, the 1960s was an age of ecumenism that had begun when Pope John XXIII convened Vatican II and opened the doors to dialogue with Protestants and those of other faith traditions. When his successor Paul VI continued leading the Church in that direction, it seemed that harmonious cooperation and religious conciliation might be achievable. Some Catholics, at least, enthusiastically embraced the possibility.

In our weekly C.C.D. class, the topic of ecumenism inevitably arose. It sparked a lively discussion until Sister Saint Agnes applied the brakes. "Ecumenical discussion is good. Talking with Protestants is fine. But don't ever go into a Protestant church."

Stunned silence followed. The teens weighed the nun's words, then let loose their objections. "Why not? What do you mean?"

With an air of certainty, she warned us, "You must never set foot in a Protestant church. Once you enter, they will never let you leave."

From deep within me, I knew her claim was false. It was absurd. More than that, it was sinister. According to this nun, Protestants were still the enemy.

That was the moment I realized that not everything spoken by priests and nuns, and perhaps not even by the Pope himself, was the truth. Every one of them was fallible. That's when I realized that I couldn't count on anyone other than myself to determine what is true.

My conscious, deliberate search for deeper religious understanding—and for a more satisfying religious community—began when I realized that nuns, priests, and the Catholic Church were all fallible. Years earlier, the parking lot incident had already suggested to me that Catholics might not be the *people of God*. The disconnect between doctrine and reality had been jarring. Catholics seemed to equate living a godly life with the observance of ritual, while they ignored Jesus's counsel that we "love one another."[6]

---

[6] *John* 13:34

Perhaps I was expecting too much. Regardless, I didn't give up on the idea that *somewhere* this people of God must exist.

The concept was compelling. It had been a component of my forgotten "dream" and kept nagging at my subconscious.

The idea continued to evolve in my mind, resonating with my readings about benevolent aliens. I was drawn to the possibility of transcending humanity's ignorance, creating a better world, and living in peace. Perhaps these people of God might exist … in a *different* church or religion.

But which church? Which religion?

When I considered the familiar options, the various denominations of Christianity, it was mind-boggling. They all differed from one another in doctrine and practice. Obviously, they couldn't *all* be right. And how could I possibly study all of them, to find which one had "the truth"?

That's when I had a clarifying thought: *all* the Christian denominations, either directly or indirectly, owed their existence to or had their origin in Roman Catholicism. They either sprang directly from Catholicism or, indirectly, from one another. *Thus,* I reasoned, *if Catholicism is flawed or in error, then they must all be flawed.*

In one swoop, I eliminated them all from consideration. In my search, I would have to go back in time. I would have to examine religion *prior to* Catholicism.

Because of my youth and lack of theological sophistication, it did not occur to me to simply back away from organized religion and begin with an examination of Jesus himself, of his life and teachings. If I had done so, I would have come to my own conclusions, without the intervention or interpretation of organized religion. But that approach did not occur to me. Instead, I decided to start with the religion that came *prior to* Jesus, the religion that *anticipated* the messiah. *Perhaps the truth lay in Judaism*, I thought.

I was impressed by the piety embodied in Jewish practice and tradition. Even everyday activities like cooking, eating, and dressing were accompanied by prayer and the inclusion of God. The Sabbath was strictly observed as a day in attendance to God alone. Perhaps these were the people I was looking for.

I spoke with my priest about it. I shared with Father Mike my thoughts on Judaism and about the possibility of conversion. He listened carefully. He seemed to respect my reasoning. "But," he concluded, "you need to be aware that although you may convert to the Jewish faith, you will never be truly accepted as a Jew. Converts are welcome, but you must be born a Jew to be considered truly Jewish. You will always be an outsider."

I believed him and was discouraged. If Judaism would not unconditionally embrace a convert, then although they may have been the chosen people of the Torah, they could not be the same people of God whom I was seeking. A loving

God, in my view, would fully embrace anyone who sought union with Him, who sought to live as His child.

Nevertheless, my world gradually broadened. In middle school and high school, I studied side by side with people of other faiths. In particular, I was impressed by my Jewish teachers and classmates. They were exemplary and altruistic human beings. They kept my interest in Judaism alive.

My Home Town

G rowing up, I never thought of Lewiston as special, but in many ways Lewiston was and is unique. It is Maine's second-largest city and a melting pot of nationalities. Even now, it has the largest Franco-American population of any city in the United States, many of whom still speak French and are proud of their ancestry and culture.

For centuries, Maine was home to the Androscoggin, the Arosaguntacook tribe of the Abenaki nation. Then the English came and drove them away. The Androscoggin fled the land, the forests and rivers of Maine, and found haven in Quebec where they were welcomed by the French.

The English flourished in Maine until technology tossed everyone into the Industrial Age. Then wave after wave of immigrants arrived. The Irish, escaping potato famine, dug canals and harnessed waterfalls. They helped build the textile mills and factories to which the Quebecois, seeking jobs and better lives, then flocked. It was immigrants who made Lewiston, back then, the wealthiest city in Maine.

Yes, Lewiston was home to people of many nationalities. They started out as immigrants but soon enough melded, merged, and blended together to become neighbors, co-workers, classmates, and even spouses.

My father's cousin married an Armenian refugee of the Turkish genocide. My earth science teacher was Lithuanian. The police chief and his family, all good friends of our family, were Italian. My first job, picking strawberries, was on the farm of a Scots-Irish family. My grandparents' neighbors were Polish. And in the realm of religious identity, as I have mentioned, several of my middle and high school teachers and classmates were Jewish. Only now, as I reflect upon the past, do I realize what a kaleidoscope of nationalities and ethnicities were represented by my neighbors, classmates, and relatives.

Of course, Lewiston is not unique in that respect. Communities across America with similar heterogeneous origins have been homogenized into blended communities that are now, quite simply, American. America as a melting pot is something we should be proud of. Why fear adding more flavor and variety to the pot?

Despite its diversity, noticeably absent from the Lewiston of my youth were people of color. In the late 1960s, a few African-American families moved in. I clearly remember our parish priest, in one homily, admonishing parishioners to be more welcoming of the newcomers. Other than those few families and some students at Bates College, to the best of my knowledge there were very few African-American residents.[7]

It was in the mid-1960s that I first saw the ugly face of racism splashed across the national television news. Every evening, I watched in dismay as African-Americans in the South were brutally attacked and arrested by police for peacefully demonstrating against discrimination. I could barely believe that what I was viewing was happening here in the United States. The hateful, violent responses of grown men and women, including government authorities whom I had been raised to respect, were incomprehensible to me. Not wanting to be numbered among the haters, I resolved in my heart to be among those who live and work to end prejudice.

Because of the scarcity of African Americans in Lewiston at that time, I did not personally witness racism there; nevertheless, I became aware of another type of bigotry, anti-Semitism. Although there may have been more to it than I could fathom as a child, the anti-Semitism I observed was subtle and passive. It consisted of feelings and opinions that were rarely expressed. This was primarily, I suppose, because the bearers of the anti-Semitic bias were the underclass and the powerless, the poor immigrants who depended on their employment by businesses owned or managed by members

---

[7] Notably, Bryant Gumbel was there. I learned this many years later when, as co-host of NBC's "Today Show," he mentioned having been a student at Bates College.

of the professional and mercantile classes, who were often Jewish. Many of the factories, the paper and textile mills, and retail businesses were owned or operated by people of Jewish descent, who were also well represented among the town's doctors, lawyers, and teachers.

The resentment against the upper strata was subtle; nevertheless, it colored conversations in the homes and families of laborers. It surfaced in tired commentary about bosses who had greater wealth, were better educated, or had higher social status. It hovered in veiled glances and whispered comments that tracked the bosses as they walked through their factories overseeing their investments.

Perhaps this would have been the case regardless of the boss's religion or ethnicity, but as a teen working in one of those factories, when I saw these things, I was dismayed. The enmity between Christian and Jew seemed to me as misguided as racism. In my opinion, racial and religious bigotry were both forms of irrational hatred. Because of this, I determined that whenever and wherever possible, I would work to transform these flawed attitudes. I would prove that Christians and Jews, as well as African Americans and whites, could get along and live together peacefully, side by side.

"Truth Even unto Its Innermost Parts"

That's why Brandeis University called out to me. Named after Justice Louis Dembitz Brandeis, the first Jewish justice on the Supreme Court, the school was founded in 1948, in part to guarantee equal access to a quality education for students of Jewish descent. Even here in the United States, Jewish students were often denied admission to colleges and universities of the highest caliber.[8]

In contrast to those other institutions, Brandeis welcomed students of all creeds and ethnicities. At its core, the university rejected religious, ethnic, and racial bias and embraced qualified students without discrimination.

Moreover, to actively promote diversity, Brandeis recruited from a wide variety of classes, cultures, and religious backgrounds, and even provided generous scholarships and other forms of assistance to the underprivileged and to minorities. I was a recipient of a full

---

[8] For example, FDR "decided there were too many Jewish students at [Harvard] and helped institute a quota," according to Kenneth L. Khachigian, "Renaming John Wayne Airport."

scholarship that ensured I would have the freedom to focus on my studies and on things that were important to me.

Given the circumstances, attending Brandeis would be an ideal way for me to demonstrate to my family—as well as to myself—that Christians and Jews could live together in peace. On such a campus, I would live a life free from prejudice, a life of harmony between and among traditional adversaries, a life that demonstrated that peace on earth was possible.

The campus was located in a suburb of Boston, Massachusetts, which was a relatively long way from my home, sociologically and geographically. For the first time, I would live in a world apart from my family, friends, and the beloved Maine environment in which I had grown up. Attending Brandeis represented breaking away from my past; it was an immersion into a wider, even more diversified world.

The school attracted me for yet another reason. Its motto, "Truth even unto its innermost parts," was compelling. It rekindled in me the spark of my earlier thirst for truth, which I thought had died. Because I had been unable to find satisfactory answers about God, by the time I was a high school senior I had become virtually agnostic. Now the mere existence of Brandeis University and its motto reminded me that truth was, in fact, a worthy pursuit.

Not only did Brandeis hold the promise of facilitating my spiritual quest and supporting my desire to promote intercultural and interreligious harmony, but also on the academic level its pre-medical program had an excellent reputation. Since I intended to become a doctor, Brandeis seemed the all-around perfect place for me.

Although the pre-med curriculum was demanding, I managed to at least give a nod to my quest by enrolling in a philosophy class as part of the humanities requirements. I'll never forget the wry smile on my professor's face. On that first day of class, Professor Greenberg moved around the conference table, asking each student to explain why he or she had chosen to enroll in his "Introduction to Philosophy" class.

Because I was shy and reserved, I was nearly the last to speak. The other students were sophisticated, articulate, and intellectual. Their reasons for taking the class sounded so elevated and grandiose. In contrast to them I felt out of place, a plain-spoken girl from a relatively underprivileged family. I wasn't even sophisticated enough to be embarrassed by my answer, "I'm taking this class because I'm looking for truth."

A few students snickered. The professor smiled a broad—but benevolent—smile. He opened his still-smiling mouth to speak, eyes twinkling. But he could only shake his head and laugh gently. He had not anticipated such an answer. The students misread his reaction, and more of them snickered. I felt humiliated but wasn't sure why.

Then inspiration poured down and the professor spoke. The laughing students were cut short when Professor

Greenberg used my response to segue into his introduction to the course. After all, the essence of philosophy is the love of wisdom. Philosophy as well as religion represents humanity's search for truth, the purpose of life, the differentiation between good and evil, and other matters of ultimate importance.

To my surprise, I had been vindicated.

The Brandeis Culture

In spite of my underlying spiritual goals, my four years of college were largely consumed by academic study and part-time jobs, leaving little time for contemplation of religion and spirituality. Nevertheless, I had enriching encounters within the diversity that was the Brandeis population, including my Jewish friends. Through conversation, observation, and other forms of interaction, I was able to learn much about Jewish culture and religion.

Jewish culture was in the air. It included stories and biblical allusions that were sometimes triggered by modern-day parallels, by theological debates among Jewish sectarians, or by something as seemingly insignificant as the meaning of a person's Hebrew name. In intimate as well as public settings, students were drawn to somber discussions of the Holocaust, or to passionately shared news or commentary about current events, especially when it came to Arab-Israeli relations.[9]

Within the Jewish demographic, I discovered a spectrum of distinctions about which I had been previously unaware. There were secular Jews as well as those from a variety of Orthodox and Reform traditions.

My neighbors in the dorm taught me Jewish songs and how to play the recorder, a traditional instrument. On quiet evenings one could hear, from time to time gently wafting on the breeze, the sound of recorders softly fluting melodies like "By the Waters of Babylon," one of my favorites.

One highlight for me was an unforgettable Passover Seder with Jane and her family. She was a quiet student whose family lived in the Boston area, not far from campus. We had befriended one another, and she and her family had welcomed me into their home to celebrate the Seder. Her parents were warm and gracious. Perhaps Jane had already shared with them about my interest in Judaism. As we prepared for the Seder, they patiently answered my questions. Then we sat, and the parents began officiating the ceremonial meal.

I had read books by Leon Uris and others in which Jewish customs or traditions are depicted. In high school, I had taught myself the Hebrew alphabet and how to read

---

[9] This was 1970-1974 and tensions in the Middle East were still high following the 1967 Six-Day War.

Hebrew words, although I knew the meaning of only a few of them.

The family began the Seder in Hebrew with the singing of the "Four Questions." [10] After each question and answer, Jane's parents repeated in English for my benefit. That's when I recognized the familiar "How is this night different from all other nights?" which initiates the telling of the story of the exodus from Egypt.

I much appreciated Jane's family for including me in this intimate sharing of the ancient tradition that recalls God's promises to the Hebrew people. An unforgettable part of the Seder for me was the revelation that Jewish people await the return of the prophet Elijah as a precursor to the coming messiah. In preparation for welcoming Elijah, a chair and a place setting are reserved at the table. A door is left open for his entrance.

That night, I became one in heart with the children of Israel. Together, we fervently hoped that Elijah would come.

In addition to my Jewish friends and acquaintances at Brandeis were Christians, practitioners of other world religions, atheists, and agnostics. The school was a diverse, blended community where every race, many nationalities, and a broad spectrum of ideological and political beliefs and socioeconomic backgrounds were represented. There at Brandeis, we were all together.

---

[10] "What are the answers to the Four Questions?"

The world of Brandeis was so different from the one in which I had grown up. It more accurately represented the wider world of humanity. As such, it helped me to develop a higher consciousness, one that embraced a universal brotherhood which, as I have come to feel, has always been the intention of the divine mind.

To me, this was heaven. This was how things were supposed to be.

Close Encounters

By the end of my junior year, for a number of reasons I had turned away from the idea of medical school. Sensing that my calling might lie elsewhere, I began to consider other options. I broadened my interests and nurtured my artistic side by taking a few humanities classes.

In a writing class, I invested a great deal of time and thought on an essay about the wisdom—and even the necessity—of having a moral code to live by. I came to the conclusion that it was people's wrong choices that led to the proliferation of human suffering. Because of that, I saw the value of being able to distinguish good from evil. Once again, I was beginning to reflect on these and other fundamental concerns.

Nevertheless, toward the end of my senior year it appeared that I had failed in my quest to find God, higher truth, and that ideal community, the people of God. Of course, in hindsight, I see that my search had had serious limitations. For one thing, it had been primarily intellectual. I had not given much thought to prayer or to spiritual discipline as possible ways of finding God or of receiving answers to my questions.

Occasionally, I would peruse a copy of the New Testament that my grandmother Éliane had given me. Although my mind was unclear about whether or not God existed, my heart still longed for God. One day I simply called out, "God, even though I don't believe in you, I wish you *did* exist."

It was shortly after that prayer that I began to see things that I hadn't noticed before. Beside the pond in the quadrangle were people at information tables. Every day, clean-cut men and women staffed those tables, speaking earnestly with students and sharing their literature. Every day, through the panoramic windows of the dining hall, I watched them and wondered: *Who are these people? And what are they doing?* Day after day I felt an urge to go out there and talk with them, to find out what they were about, but each time, my cautious side won out.

Then one day I went to the Student Union Cafe for a late lunch. No sooner had I sat down when two clean-cut people approached me. With a heavy French accent, the young man asked politely, "May we join you?"

They were complete strangers. Without pause and to my own surprise, I blurted out cheerfully, "Sure! As long as you don't try to convert me!"

The man smiled and exchanged a glance with his companion, a young Japanese woman. They sat. Neither spoke English very well. In fact, Hiromi didn't attempt to speak at all. She simply smiled and nodded whenever, in the course of the conversation, I looked over at her.

The man's accent intrigued me. I spoke some French. Here was an opportunity to practice my language skills and to help him out at the same time. Since Hiromi didn't seem to understand English, I invited Roger to converse in French. He seemed relieved. Hiromi continued to smile and nod.

My French skills turned out to be deficient. My French was Canadian, quotidian, and rusty. His was Parisian and current. To make matters worse, he was talking about abstract things like God and theology, and for me that lexicon was alien. Many times, I had to ask him to slow down, to repeat, or to explain something in simpler terms.

When my lunch break was over and it was time to return to my campus job, I thanked them and began to excuse myself. That's when Roger hastily beseeched me to attend a lecture, in Boston, that evening. I was not expecting such an invitation. He was, after all, a stranger.

I responded vaguely that I would consider attending a lecture, but not tonight. Visibly disappointed, he again pleaded with me to come that very night. I smiled, "Maybe another time. Thanks for sharing with me." And I left.

A few days later I was in my dorm room, absorbed in a book on psychology, trying to analyze some peculiarities of a friend whose father had labeled him a sociopath. Was that diagnosis justified? I wanted to help.

All of a sudden, I couldn't keep my mind on the book. An overpowering urge to go outside came over me. Through the open window the beautiful green field, the warm air and the sunshine called to me. Other students were out there sunning themselves, sprawled on the grass, reading or just lounging and enjoying the warm spring day. I gave in and decided to continue reading outside, on that grassy common.

Barely had I settled on my patch of grass when I looked up and saw, in the distance, two men standing on the crest of the hill. When I looked again, they were walking down the hill and, in spite of all the other students scattered about, I felt that they were walking toward me. Unexpectedly, my heart leapt in joy. *They've come for me!*

In that moment, I had remembered the altruistic aliens, the extraterrestrials whom, when I was young, I had wanted to join. I had waited for them, looking to the sky whenever an unusual sound would echo through the hills and valleys near my home. And then, of course, I had grown up. I no longer believed in aliens, and I was embarrassed to recall my childish fantasy.

And yet, what had made me think of the benevolent aliens when I saw those men? Besides, what made me so sure they were approaching *me*?

But they were. As I carefully watched them, they were definitely looking back at me; and they didn't waver or stop until they stood directly in front of me where I sat on the warm spring grass, psychology book still open in my hands.

"Hello! What are you reading?" Tom asked by way of introduction. I explained, in depth. And thus began our conversation.

Tom and Daniel had no idea that just a few days earlier I had met two of their colleagues in the cafe. On my part, I was relieved that Tom spoke unaccented American English and that his emphasis was less theological and more down-to-earth. He talked about the "Unified Family," the community to which he belonged in California, and their plan to create a peaceful society and world. As it turned out, the young people I had been meeting were part of an international crusade.

Daniel had a thick French accent, so he mostly listened to our spirited conversation. What Tom was saying, not only about the ideal world but also about God—because I had mentioned wanting proof of God's existence—intrigued me, especially as Tom's approach was fresh and novel. Not only that, but he confidently affirmed that their lecture series would definitively prove God's existence.

That got my attention. I had never before encountered a person or teaching that claimed to be able to *prove* God's existence. That alone was worth a visit to their church. Because this teaching might answer my questions, I agreed to go with them that very evening.

I was mindful of my cautious side, so when they suggested that I meet them in the quad at five o'clock, I replied, "Instead of that, would you please come to my dorm room and pick me up? Otherwise, I might change my mind."

Thus, promptly at five o'clock, Tom and Daniel knocked on my door. We walked to the parking lot, chatting along the way, and joined a number of other students who were coming along as well. We climbed into a van and drove off.

Attached to the vehicle's front console was the photo of an Asian couple. For some reason, the man's face seemed familiar. I stared at it for a while before asking, "Who is that?"

"That's our founder, Reverend Moon, and his wife."

"Ah. I see. Thanks."

In good time, we arrived at the church in Boston. As it turned out, they had spoken truly. The lecture was amazing. The teaching was comprehensive and coherent. It was consistent with all that I knew to be true. There were no contradictions, no gaps, no "mysteries."

Based on that initial presentation, I felt that this might be the truth I had been seeking. Issues that I had pondered for years were being addressed. The introductory lecture had not yet proven God's existence, but it did present God and the universe in a compelling, reasonable light. And more was promised. This *Divine Principle* teaching, an entire series of presentations, certainly seemed worth hearing. I was eager to come back for more.

In response to my questions, I was told that the presentation on the origin of evil would explain what had gone wrong at the start of human history and why humankind has been unable thus far to achieve a world of goodness. I was so eager to hear that second presentation that I returned the very next night. But instead of a presentation on the nature of evil, the lecturer gave the same introductory lecture he had given the previous evening. When he finished, I complained. "I thought this lecture was going to explain the origin of evil."

"Oh, sorry! To hear *that* presentation, or any other in the series, you'll have to attend a weekend workshop. On weeknights, we present only this introduction."

Unfortunately, my schedule did not allow for a weekend workshop. I was preparing to graduate and to return to Maine to begin a new job up in Calais, on the border with Canada.

My First Workshop

When I had decided against medical school, I did not yet know what I wanted to do with my life. Until I could figure that out, I would need employment. Regardless of how I earned money, I thought that the Maine coast would be an idyllic location for me to explore my artistic side. I'd be immersed in Maine's natural beauty as I tried to figure out what I really wanted to do.

I took a civil service exam and landed a job as an immigration inspector in Calais. While preparing for the move, I was living with some cousins in Auburn. One day, the phone rang. It was for me.

"Hello! Eez zeez Poleen?" asked a man in a heavy French accent.

"Roger! What a surprise! How are you?"

After some small talk, only half of which I understood because of the accent and the static on the phone line, Roger brought up his reason for calling. "Zer eez a workshop ... zeez weekend ... Reek Hunter ... Portland. Weell you come?"

"Portland? Oh, yes, it's only thirty minutes from here. But I don't have a car. I don't know how I could get there."

"Reek will peek you up and drive you to zee workshop."

I had two more weeks before I had to be in Calais. I already had my uniform, a room to rent, and everything else I needed. *I've got time. Why not?*

"Yes. I can go. How do I contact Rick?"

Roger provided the information and I called Rick. On the appointed day, my bag was packed. Rick arrived, clean-cut and well-mannered; he made a favorable impression on my cousin and me. As we chatted comfortably around the kitchen table, he explained about the workshop … in Barrytown, New York.

"What? I thought the workshop was in Portland!"

"Portland? Oh! No. Sorry! Our church is in Portland, but we're driving to Barrytown for the workshop. It's about a five-hour drive."

I was a bit disappointed. Barrytown was pretty far away. Still, I had the time. *Besides, this might be my only chance to hear this "Principle" they talk about, so why not?*

"Oh, alright! I'm packed anyway. What's the difference, Portland or New York? Let's go!"

The Divine Principle

The *Divine Principle* workshop was held on the campus of what had once been St. Joseph's Normal Institute operated by the Christian Brothers. The Unification movement had only recently purchased the property from them.

The workshop schedule consisted of songs and prayer, lectures and discussions, recreation, meals, and sleep. The presentations were everything that had been promised … and more. After years of searching and then resigning myself to first agnosticism and, eventually, atheism, I was at last finding satisfactory explanations regarding God, religion, and human history. God's existence now seemed plausible.

The *Principle* clarified the nature of God and how to relate to Him. Not only that, but the origin and nature of evil were explained satisfactorily, showing how and why the solution to evil lies in human hands … with divine help. It was comprehensible and reasonable. There were no gaps in logic; there was no need to accept "mysteries" on blind faith.

In addition to hearing presentations, participants were encouraged to reflect, meditate, and pray. Prayer, in the form of honest conversation with God, was modelled, which was especially helpful for those of us who had come from traditions of reciting formulaic prayers.

The presentations at the two-day workshop were compelling, once again suggesting to me that the *Divine Principle* might indeed be that truth I was seeking. At the close of the weekend, participants were invited to stay for a more extensive, seven-day workshop.

I was eager to stay. What I had learned so far had been mind-blowing. If this was what I thought it was, how could I say no?

The schedule for the seven-day workshop was similar to that of the previous two days. As promised, the central assertions of the *Principle* were explained in greater detail and at greater depth. In the process, the Bible became more comprehensible to me. That alone would have been a significant achievement.

With each presentation, I had the same reaction. Every element struck a chord; every word rang true. The teaching made sense, not only of God and religion, but of the entire range of human history and experience. The *Principle* was an all-encompassing matrix into which everything important fit.

It clearly answered, to my utmost satisfaction, essential theological issues that I had pondered for years. For example,

If a good and loving God is at the same time almighty, then why is there evil and suffering in the world?

If the crucifixion and resurrection brought salvation to humanity, then why is the world not yet saved?

Why is a second coming necessary?

In these brief pages, I can offer only a taste of the *Divine Principle.*[11] I can only hint at how, although biblically based, it is revolutionary.

The presentation on the origin of evil was particularly enlightening. It touched on problematic issues of human nature and history, revealing how an initial misstep has continued to reverberate, having consequences down to the present time.

The symbolic nature of the biblical story about original sin was unlocked. The original mistaken act involved a misuse of love, which thwarted the fulfillment of the Creator's blueprint for human life.

The lecturer used vivid examples to illustrate the nature of true love. It became obvious to me that what we call "love" often falls short of the ideal. When people use others for their own pleasure or gain, that is selfish, false love. In contrast, true love is sacrificial, unselfish, and focused on the welfare of others.

I had not previously considered the importance of being able to distinguish genuine love from false versions of it. Sex without commitment and responsibility has nothing to do

---

[11] Sun Myung Moon, *Exposition of the Divine Principle.*

with love. So-called "free sex" and narcissistic sexual practices bring us nowhere near the genuine love that God intends for us.

The presentations also clarified why God's original vision or ideal for human existence has not yet been fulfilled. From the moment of our primordial mistake, our Heavenly Parent has been guiding us toward paths of restoration. But restoration requires human cooperation, which has not always been forthcoming. Fortunately for us, God has not given up and will not give up. His hope for a fully restored humanity is ongoing, no matter how long it takes.

Some of the most puzzling theological issues for me had involved Jesus. I had often wondered why God would send a messiah only to have him killed. If rejection and execution were the goal, why would God have worked for millennia to prepare a foundation whereby the people of Israel would hunger for—and embrace—their messiah? A messiah could easily have been crucified without all that advance preparation.

That's why I was relieved to learn, from the clear and logical perspective of the *Principle*, that the rejection and execution of God's son was not the original plan for salvation.[12] Jesus himself had clarified that it was God's will that we *believe* in him. When the people had asked, "What

---

[12] If the executioners were accomplishing God's will, why would Jesus pray, "Father, forgive them; for they know not what they do"? (*Luke* 23:34)

must we do, to be doing the works of God?" Jesus responded, "This is the work of God, that you believe in him whom he has sent."[13] His entire ministry was aimed at convincing people to accept and embrace him as Lord.[14]

Nevertheless, in the end, Jesus' crucifixion became an offering on behalf of a humanity that had rejected him. Because he gave his life willingly, and because he died while loving and praying for his enemies, a path for salvation on the spiritual level was opened. Salvation on the physical, earthly plane, however, would have to await a "second coming," a return of God's son to earth.

Why is that? What was Jesus meant to accomplish over the course of his earthly life?

As I discovered, the goal of both God and God's son, then as well as now, is nothing short of complete salvation. This means the restoration of humanity back to a life lived according to the original divine blueprint. Jesus was meant to model for us a life of perfected humanity; he intended to show us how to live as God's children.[15]

For me this was all so logical. There was nothing irrational or magical about it. As the new Adam, Jesus came

---

[13] *John* 6: 28-29.

[14] From this I learned that the accomplishment of God's will depends upon human cooperation. The goal of restoring humanity back to God's original ideal has not changed, but when we don't cooperate, God has to revise His plan for how to achieve this.

[15] *Romans* 8:14-17.

to do what the first Adam had failed to do: establish a model, sinless, godly family.

Due to their initial misstep, the first Adam and Eve had unwittingly betrayed God's plan and had become *false* parents and *false* ancestors. Consequently, they led humanity away from our Heavenly Parent and toward evil. Because of this, we need *true* parents ... who will re-connect us with God as our Heavenly Parent.

Thus, Jesus came as a new, sinless Adam. [16] He was to become our *true* parent and model for us the way to cast off our fallen nature and cultivate our innate divinity. "Be perfect as your heavenly Father is perfect" is what he instructed.[17] As the model man, Jesus was to have set the standard for living a sinless life.

Moreover, if God would send a new Adam to guide the process of renewing humanity and bringing us back to His bosom, would He not also send a new Eve? If there is an Only Begotten Son, should there not also be an Only Begotten Daughter? After all, based on the ideal of God's creation, as expressed in the book of *Genesis*, a family consists of a mother as well as a father.[18]

The anticipated "Marriage of the Lamb" in the book of *Revelation* refers to the actual marriage between the new

---

[16] *1 Corinthians* 15: 45-49; 15: 21-22; *Romans* 5:14. Keep in mind that the original Adam was also the "son of God," according to *Luke* 3:38.

[17] *Matthew* 5:48.

[18] *Genesis* 1:27-28; 2:18, 21-24.

Adam and a new Eve.[19] That is because the purpose of the Second Coming is to complete the original messianic mission. In other words, the coming messiah and his bride, as God's true son and daughter, will replace the fallen Adam and Eve to become the *true* parents of humanity. Through engrafting to them, humanity will be born anew as God's children and, in this way, a new history—a new heaven and earth—will begin.[20]

Over the course of the workshop, whenever I put on the brakes and thought, *Wait a minute! This is too good to be true,* God reached out and confirmed for me the truth of the teaching. Throughout those seven days, I had deep, personal experiences of God.

The workshop was the turning point of my life. The *Divine Principle* was the "speaking plainly" that Jesus had promised. It was the truth that the "Spirit of truth" was to reveal.[21]

Importantly, I was relieved (as well as joyful) to discover that I could believe in a God and in a process of human history and salvation that was clear, reasonable, and internally consistent. It meant that I could lead an enlightened life as well as a godly one.

---

[19] *Revelation* 19: 7-9; 21: 9-10; 22:17.
[20] *Romans* 8:23.
[21] *John* 16: 12-13, 25.

The Heart of God

By far the most important aspect of that *Divine Principle* workshop was that I came to know God in a new way. Not only was I convinced intellectually of His existence, but through grace I was able to directly and personally experience Him as the loving, divine essence at the center of the cosmos.

As I awoke to this new reality, like a baby I took my first wobbly steps in the direction of getting to know this God as my Heavenly Parent. I was relieved and happy to leave behind unsatisfactory concepts of an almighty and exacting judge who punishes the wicked. Instead, I came to know the origin of the universe as a loving Parent who cannot rest until each and every child—without exception—joyfully returns to His bosom.

Yes, hell and suffering exist—on earth as well as in the spiritual realm—but as it turns out these are *not* divine punishments. It is we humans, not God, who create our own misery. Unhappiness and suffering are the consequences of ignorant and self-centered choices. That means we have the power, with God's help, to change it all, to make a new reality.

Moreover, because our spirit is eternal, we can learn and grow even after our physical life has ended. Opportunities exist, even in the spiritual realm, to heal our hearts and to restore our relationships with God and with other people. But it is far more difficult to do so in the spiritual realm. That's why it is wise to grow our spirit and our capacity for altruistic love while we are alive on earth, in our physical bodies.

Once again, it is not God who assigns people to heaven or hell. After earthly life, we enter the spiritual realm and automatically find ourselves in an environment compatible with our current level of spiritual development. That's why it is in our best interest, while we are alive on earth, to expand our ability to genuinely love others, so that after death we will dwell in an environment of greater love and peace, an environment comprised of people who are capable of giving and receiving God's abundant, unconditional, unselfish love.

The *Divine Principle* is a teaching of total salvation. No one is damned to eternal suffering. Like the prodigal son, eventually all will be healed and restored to the loving parental heart of God. Until that day, the Heavenly Parent does not rest and cannot be joyful.

How can a loving Parent be happy if even one child suffers? If human parents, imperfect as we are, feel grief over the suffering of our children, how much greater is the

Heavenly Parent's sorrow? Because God intensely loves each and every one of us, His heart is full of pain and sorrow over the misery of His children.

Beyond learning of the Creator's essence as a Parent with a heart of unconditional love, I came to see Him as a sentient being who exists as a harmonious union of internal character and external form, and of masculinity and femininity *(yang* and *yin)*.[22] Humans, created in the image and likeness of God, also possess these characteristics. Because of the fundamental masculinity and femininity that comprise the divine nature, as well as the parental heart that motivates the Creator, we can relate to God as "Our Mother" as well as "Our Father."[23]

Of course, God has no body; nevertheless, the divine essential masculinity and essential femininity are reflected in the creation, embodied in substantial beings.

> God said, "Let us make man in our image, after our likeness…." So God created man in his own image, in the image of God he created him; male and female he created them.[24]

---

[22] Because God has both internal character and external form, I came to understand His external form as the primal Energy of the cosmos.

[23] As a reminder of God's perfectly harmonized dual feminine and masculine natures, Unificationists refer to God as our "Heavenly Parent."

[24] *Genesis* 1: 26-27.

Moreover, to the extent that we perfect ourselves, we resonate with and embody our Creator's loving parental heart.[25] When that happens, people can experience God through their interactions with others.[26] People can experience divine love, mercy, and compassion through the loving kindness of those who reach out to comfort or help them.

Based on my account thus far, the reader might assume that my experience at the *Divine Principle* workshop was purely intellectual, but that is far from the case. My experiences were richly multi-dimensional and included events of a deeply spiritual and powerful nature. In fact, it was through prayer and revelation that I was able to experience God's *personhood*.

For example, on one occasion as I processed what I was hearing, I came to a roadblock. The lecturer had been repeatedly referring to "God's heart." The concept was new to me.

What does he mean by "God's heart"? In sincere prayer I asked God, addressing Him in the personal manner I had observed the Unification Church members using. "Dear Heavenly Father, what do they mean by *God's heart*? What

---

[25] "You, therefore, must be perfect, as your heavenly Father is perfect." (*Matthew* 5:48)

[26] *Namaste*, a greeting that means "I salute the divine within you," holds that special meaning for me.

are they talking about? Please help me to understand this …
to understand You."

That night, God answered my prayer.

While I slept, I had an out-of-body experience. An angel
came. He stood at the window at the foot of my bed in the
dormitory. He informed me that he had been sent to escort
me to God, who would directly answer my question.

In the manner of Ebenezer Scrooge and the ghost of
Christmas past, we stood on the ledge of the open window.
When I took the angel's hand, we flew out into the night sky.
We traveled a vast distance into the depths of the cosmos.
The angel brought me to the very center, which was God.

There, God said to me, "You have asked to know My
heart and so you shall. But you will experience My suffering
for only an instant because more than that would be
unbearable for you."

Then I was drawn into or melded with God's heart,
feeling as God felt. And He said, "This is my pain."

I felt His agony. With my entire being I felt His aching
sorrow. The divine Parent's anguish over the suffering—
mental, spiritual, physical—of each and every human life
was overwhelming, crushing, unbearable.

He had spoken truly. I felt that I would surely die if I had
to endure it for even one more fraction of a second.

After a while, after I had caught my breath and
composed myself, God said, "And this is my heart of love."
Once again, my heart melded with God's, and this time I felt

73

the Creator's unconditional and boundless love, the heart of a perfect Parent … for me and for every other human being. And that, too, was incredibly intense. The magnitude of God's love was boundless; I felt I would explode.

"Now you know my heart," said God.

I awoke in tears.

I had experienced God as my own loving Parent and Creator, infinitely loving and embracing, infinitely forgiving. And the Heavenly Parent's heart of love was bursting with empathy, aching with compassion for the pain His billions of children endure as they live and suffer in ignorance.

Not only that, but imagine the heart of a parent whose child is blind to the parent's love, ignorant of and indifferent to the sacrifices the parent makes on behalf of the child, and unaware of the parent's hopes and dreams for the child's eternal happiness. Such a sorrowful parent is God.

This was the starting point for me. For the first time, I was aware that God has feelings, intense feelings, of sorrow as well as love and joy. I learned that God suffers even more than we do because He shares the pain and suffering of each and every individual on the planet.

Now when I think of God, I'm aware of the Creator's parental love and the crushing agony that comes with such love. Our Heavenly Parent watches anxiously as His children stumble in ignorance, oblivious to their Parent's love and even to His existence, unaware that their own ignorant choices are the cause of their suffering.

Thus, to truly know God is to know His suffering heart. The author of the *Divine Principle* conveys this when he says

> … God experiences the emotions of deepest sorrow and greatest joy. It is not true that God has only joyful and pleasant emotions. When He is sorrowful, His sorrow is deep and wide, beyond what any human being can fathom.[27]

> I came to learn that God is not a Being sitting on a throne of glory and honor. Rather, He is a God of sadness, lamentation and anguish, endeavoring to save His children who fell and plunged into hell.[28]

This parental, loving God will go to the bottom of hell to reach His children. Thus, to liberate hell is to liberate God, who will rest only after each child has been restored.

[27] Sun Myung Moon, "The God of Heart," 53, #1.
[28] Moon, "The Path of Humanity," 1436.

The Second Coming

Despite the logic of the teachings and the abundance of God's signs and assurances to me throughout the workshop, I had to grapple with a final hurdle. I had heard all the presentations of the *Principle*. I had experienced episodes of doubt and cross-examination. Along the way, when I had asked God for clarification and confirmation, God had responded, clearly and personally. I could only conclude that the *Divine Principle* was indeed the truth I had been seeking.

But there was that final hurdle. Based on the evidence, it seemed that the messiah himself might be on the earth. I wanted to retreat to a quiet place, to think and pray about this. I needed to talk to God in private.

The opportunity for this arose when the workshop was on break time. Out on the field, people were gathering for a volleyball game. Since I was reserved about doing spiritual things like praying in public, I didn't want to reveal my actual purpose for wanting to be alone. I told a staff person that I was going for a walk.

The campus was large and spacious. Up above was a beautiful blue dome of sky and a golden sun. Warm May breezes wafted through and above the ancient trees and along the rolling hills and the vast fields of tall grass. And along the western border of the campus flowed the glittering Hudson River.

But I was blind to the beauty. My heart was bursting. Barely breathing, I choked back tears and ran toward the open fields. Once out of range, when my privacy was assured, the dam burst and I called out to God, sobbing, walking, and praying all at the same time. When I was even farther out into the field, I dropped to my knees in the tall grass. In tears, I begged God to guide me.

I looked back on the events. At every turn of the workshop, I had analyzed and re-analyzed the material. With God and with people I had debated and weighed the evidence from many angles. I had considered how traditional Christian doctrines had been formulated and why theologians had interpreted scripture in the manner that they had.

At every turn, the lecturers and staff had patiently responded to my questions and concerns. Even more importantly, God had many times intervened and dispelled my apprehensions, showing me grace and giving me signs of His presence and love. And yet here I was, despite all that, still entertaining doubt.

"God, I'm so sorry! You showed me everything. You answered my questions. You gave me proof. Yet here I am, once again, wavering."

Over and over again I apologized for my skepticism. "That's just the way I am," I lamented. "If the messiah himself were to appear in front of me, I would probably not believe it. I'm so sorry!"

I poured out my heart. God had to know that, despite my hesitation, I was doing my best. I simply needed help with this final issue. *Has the messiah returned? Is he here now, living among us?*

When I had nothing left to say and no more tears to weep, a peace came over me. I returned to the main building.

In an otherwise empty classroom, I was greeted by Cheri, who had joined the church just one week earlier. A kind, generous person, it seemed that she had adopted me as her little sister. Now she could hardly contain her excitement. "Father—I mean Reverend Moon—is here!"

The founder of the Unification Church had dropped by for a visit. Cheri wanted to catch a glimpse of him as he was leaving. She had been looking for me to come along. She took my hand and we ran through the building. We stopped at a small driveway by the kitchen door. Parked there was a car with its rear door open. Several people stood around respectfully.

Reverend Moon was standing beside the car, his hand resting on the open door. He was talking and gesturing. His back was turned to me. The most peculiar thing was that I couldn't see his head. It seemed that a white fluffy cloud was obscuring my view. No matter how he moved, the cloud surrounded his head. Even when he turned around, the cloud was there, hiding his face.

I blinked. *Why can't I see him?* No matter how hard I tried, the cloud was there. I could not see beyond it or through it.

I looked down at his feet for a moment as I tried to make sense of the phenomenon. As though he heard my thoughts, he turned to face me. When I looked up again, the cloud was gone. I saw his face.

I looked into his eyes. There was no end to their depth. It was like looking into the cosmos. And from somewhere deep within me, without my thinking or willing it, rose the clear affirmation, *It's him.*

Sun Myung Moon

When I first heard the *Divine Principle*, I had no idea of the price Reverend Moon had paid to receive this new wine, the "making plain" that Jesus had promised regarding the parables and figures of the Bible.[29] It was only over time that I learned the background of his story.

It was dawn on Easter Sunday in 1935 when Jesus first came to the young man. He had just spent the night in prayer atop a mountain, begging God for a way to ease the world's suffering, including that of his homeland of Korea, which was enduring a brutal occupation by the Japanese empire.

In his memoir, Reverend Moon recounts that Jesus

> ...appeared in an instant, like a gust of wind, and said to me, "God is in great sorrow because of the pain of humankind. You must take on a special mission on earth having to do with Heaven's work."

> That morning, I saw clearly the sorrowful face of Jesus. I heard his voice clearly. The experience of witnessing the manifestation of Jesus caused my body to shake

---

[29] *John* 16: 12, 25.

violently.... I was simultaneously overcome with fear so great I felt I might die and gratitude so profound I felt I might explode. Jesus spoke clearly about the work I would have to do. His words were extraordinary, having to do with saving humanity from its suffering and bringing joy to God.

My initial response was, "I can't do this. How can I do this? Why would you even give me a mission of such paramount importance?" I was truly afraid. I wanted somehow to avoid this mission, and I clung to the hem of his clothing and wept inconsolably.[30]

Though feeling unworthy and inadequate for such a task, the fifteen-year-old gradually came to understand that if God had called him, he must obey. From that time, Sun Myung Moon walked a lonely, suffering path.

For the next nine years, he searched for answers to fundamental biblical questions. Witnesses have testified that at times he prayed, sobbing uncontrollably, for days at a time. Through his communication with God, the saints, and with Jesus himself, he came to know the suffering heart of the Creator and the secrets of God's efforts to restore fallen humanity.

Sun Myung Moon, by then in his twenties, concluded this initial period with a forty-day fast. As Jesus had been confronted by Satan after his forty-day fast, so too the young man's understanding of the truth had to endure the challenge of Lucifer. Next, he had to face God's initial refusal to

---

[30] S.M. Moon, *Peace-Loving Global Citizen*, 50.

acknowledge his conclusions—until after he had adequately defended and upheld them. In the end Jesus himself, along with founders of other major world religions, confirmed the truth of Father Moon's findings. These became the basis of the *Divine Principle*.

Then began the next phase of the young man's ministry: to heal God's grief by sharing this knowledge with the rest of the world.[31]

In August 1945, Japan was defeated in World War II and Korea was liberated from Japanese occupation. Unfortunately, Korea was subsequently divided at the 38th parallel, and the northern portion was relinquished to communist control. In the southern part of the peninsula, now that Japanese suppression of religion was a thing of the past, Reverend Moon was free to openly begin his ministry.[32]

In June of 1946, however, he received a revelation from God: "Go across the 38th parallel! Find the people of God who are in the North."[33]

He left abruptly, considering a command from God to be a serious matter to be followed without delay. He journeyed to Pyongyang, which at that time was known as the "Jerusalem of the East" because of its vibrant

---

[31] Breen, *Sun Myung Moon*, 36-37. Breen's book depicts compelling details of this period of Father Moon's life.

[32] S.M. Moon, *Peace-Loving Global Citizen*, 82-3; Breen, 64.

[33] S.M. Moon, 84.

Christianity, which had begun to blossom again after the departure of the Japanese.[34]

In Pyongyang, Reverend Moon attended revival meetings and preached. Within a short time, he had gained recognition as a spiritual leader.[35]

At that same time, the atheistic North Korean communist government had begun to suppress the practice of religion. In August 1946, the young preacher was arrested and brought to the Daedung security police station in Pyongyang. There he met other leading Christian ministers who had also been imprisoned for their preaching.[36]

The communists charged him with espionage; they interrogated and tortured him. In the end, however, they found him innocent. On October 31, 1946, they released his near-dead body, his clothing torn and clotted with blood, to his disciples.[37] He was vomiting so much blood that his followers prepared for his funeral, but instead of dying, he was slowly nursed back to health. The effects of this—as well as of subsequent tortures—took a toll that would last throughout his life.

After his recovery, Sun Myung Moon bravely resumed teaching and preaching in North Korea. By the end of 1947, he had built a stable congregation of about forty people.

---

34 S.M. Moon, 84-5; Breen, *Sun Myung Moon,* 70.

35 S.M. Moon, 84-9; Breen, 74.

36 Moon, 89; Breen, 75-79.

37 Breen, 79-80.

Then, in February of 1948, he was arrested once again for preaching. This time, he was put on public trial. He was mocked. Observers at the trial shouted for him to be executed. He was pronounced guilty and sentenced to five years in prison.[38]

In May of that year, the twenty-eight-year-old preacher was sent to Hungnam Prison labor camp, a communist death camp. The prisoners worked at the nearby Korean Nitrogen Fertilizer factory loading bags of ammonium sulfate with bare hands until their skin melted and exposed their bones. The noxious fumes damaged their lungs. There were harsh quotas: seventy bags per person per day; one hundred thirty bags if they were being punished.[39] If the quota was not met, their meager rations—already a starvation diet—were cut in half.[40]

Father Moon has depicted the harsh circumstances in this way:

> Prisoners were ... exposed to sulfuric acid, which was used in the manufacture of ammonium sulfate.... Exposure to sulfuric acid was so harmful that it would cause hair loss and sores on our skin that oozed liquid. Most people who worked in the factory would begin vomiting blood and die after about six months. We would wear rubber pieces on our fingers for protection, but the acid would quickly wear through these. The acid fumes would also eat through our clothes, making them

---

[38] S.M. Moon, *Peace-Loving Global Citizen*, 89-91; Breen, 86-87.
[39] Breen, 92-3.
[40] S.M. Moon, *Peace-Loving Global Citizen*, 93-97.

useless, and our skin would break and bleed. In some cases, the bone would become visible. We had to continue working without so much as a day's rest, even when our sores were bleeding and oozing pus.[41]

For the first two weeks of his confinement, the young preacher resolved to help fellow prisoners by giving away half of his meager rations. He had decided that he would neither eat nor sleep except as he himself determined; he wanted to ensure that his spirit would dominate his body, regardless of the suffering involved.[42]

While undergoing these ordeals, the young Reverend Moon remained true to God and to Jesus ... *by loving his enemies.* This he did in Hungnam as well as throughout his entire life, including the time, years earlier, that he had saved the life of a man who had tortured him.[43]

Reverend Moon and other surviving prisoners escaped from Hungnam Prison on October 14, 1950 as it was being bombed by United Nations forces pressing into Korea.[44] On foot, he returned to Pyongyang to search for his former followers. Many of them had already fled south.

After forty days in Pyongyang, the preacher and his disciple Won Pil Kim, together with another former Hungnam prisoner, a Mr. Pak, headed south, again on foot.

---

[41] Moon, 96.

[42] Moon, 96-97.

[43] H.J.H. Moon, *Mother of Peace*, 268.

[44] S.M. Moon, *Peace-Loving Global Citizen*, 103-4. The Korean War began June 25, 1950 and "ended" July 27, 1953.

Because Mr. Pak's leg was broken, they pushed him along on a bicycle; at times, Reverend Moon carried him on his back. Under the adverse circumstances of the Korean War, the three made their way south and crossed the border into South Korea.[45]

After ensuring medical treatment for Mr. Pak, Reverend Moon and his disciple continued their journey south to Busan. There they built, on a precarious spot on a hillside, a small shelter made of rocks, mud, and cardboard boxes. It was there, in that humble hut, that Reverend Moon prayed continually and wrote the first draft of the *Divine Principle*.[46]

[45] S.M. Moon, 105-107.
[46] S.M. Moon, 112-113; Breen, 145.

New Life

The purpose of truth is to realize goodness.
—Sun Myung Moon

When the *Divine Principle* was shared with me, my life was transformed. As Jesus had promised, the truth had made me free.[47]

That's because truth is not just an abstract or intellectual matter. Knowing what is true also means knowing what is good and what is evil; and that kind of knowledge informs a person's choices. More often than not, people choose to do what they believe to be good.

We have the mantra, "Do the right thing." The million-dollar question is: "What *is* the right thing?" When a person can distinguish truth from falsehood, and good from evil, he or she will make better choices.

---

[47] *John* 8: 31-32.

The *Divine Principle* made more sense to me than any other religious or philosophical explanation. It was clear and cogent and, because there were no lapses of common sense or logic, there was no need to accept anything on blind faith. *Divine Principle* was quite simply the most reasonable account of God and reality, both spiritual and physical, that I had ever encountered.

By the end of the seven-day workshop, I knew that I wanted to join this people of God. When the staff members were distributing membership forms, I asked for one. In the box where it asked "Reason for Joining," I wrote simply "Because I want to help God."

I never made it to my first day as an immigration inspector in Calais. I called my supervisor to let her know that I wouldn't be taking the position after all. Using terms that I hoped she would understand, I told her that I had joined a church and had decided to become a missionary. She didn't know quite how to respond.

Joining the Unification movement was the best thing that ever happened to me. It marked my introduction to the living God and to the divine motivation behind the existence of the cosmos. Now I was able to love God with all my heart and soul and, critically important for me, all my mind.[48] The Eucharist song I had so loved as a child became reality: I

---

[48] *Mark* 12: 30.

could truly affirm that "I received the living God, and my heart is full of joy."[49]

From a practical perspective, knowledge of the *Divine Principle* changed the way I led my life. Because I was able to distinguish good from evil, I deeply repented of my prior ignorance and my poor choices. Because I could better understand human dynamics, I was able to sincerely forgive those who had harmed or wronged me in the past.

After I heard the lecture on the origin of evil, I understood why "free sex" is a harmful concept and practice. Because we are meant to exist as embodiments of the living God, promiscuous behavior is degrading to human dignity. Moreover, it shows a lack of respect toward each person involved. Finally, the practice of free sex defies God's intention for the establishment of harmonious, happy families.

As I put the *Principle* into practice, I developed spiritually and emotionally. That was to be expected because, after all, "the purpose of truth is to realize goodness."[50] For example, if I examined difficulties or challenges from a *Principle* perspective, I would experience God's presence and assistance. Such experiences confirmed for me the wisdom of living by the *Principle*.

Finally, after I had chosen to walk this path, I received a conclusive, overwhelmingly irrefutable personal

---

[49] Anonymous, "Communion Hymn."
[50] S.M. Moon, *Exposition of the Principle*, 9.

confirmation of God's presence within the Unification movement. It had to do with that "night vision," the one that I'd had as a child, where an angel revealed to me an important truth ... but then told me that my memory of it would be erased until the "right time" would arrive.

Because I had met the Unification movement through the International One World Crusade (IOWC), I had initially become part of that IOWC team. As a team, we were living in and working out of the Boston church center.

One morning as I was seated in study, the *Divine Principle* book open in my hands, it all came back to me. In one great epiphany, as though the heavens had opened, I re-experienced the entire vision. I remembered the journey with the angel, the book held open as he explained the contents of the revelation, and the discovery that Christ was on Earth and that people were working with him to build God's kingdom.

In every detail, I relived the experience, including my fervent desire to join those people and to share the good news with the world. I remembered my anguish when the angel had informed me that I would not remember any of this ... *until the time was right.*

And now the time had come. In that moment, I realized that the book in my hands, the *Divine Principle*, was the book the angel had shared with me in that night vision.

I knew that I was in the right place. In spite of the twists and turns of my young life, God had been there all along, guiding me.

How I Got to the MFT

From the start of my new life at the age of twenty-two, I experienced countless valuable lessons. For example, when I first went out with fellow missionaries to evangelize or to raise funds, the cooperation of angels and good spirits became real for me.

Because I was more comfortable with fundraising than with witnessing, I was assigned to a fundraising team.[51] Werner, our team captain, was a humble, kind-hearted elder brother from Austria. He reminded us that people in the spiritual world are eager to help us fulfill God's will and create His kingdom on earth. He explained how people in the spiritual realm benefit from supporting the good works of people on earth. For this reason, we may enlist their cooperation: we can let them know our plans and how they can assist us.

---

[51] As a child, I had sold candy bars to raise funds for my Catholic school. I had sold Girl Scout cookies. In my high school civics club, I had raised funds for an international charity.

One day, I was selling flowers at a traffic light at a busy intersection off a highway ramp in the Boston area. I decided to experiment. I hugged my bucket of flowers and prayed, trying to be sensitive to the good spirits who might be around to help. What happened next made me feel that I had succeeded.

As each car approached my intersection, every driver looked at me, eyes opened wide. He or she automatically reached for his or her wallet and gave a donation. I didn't even have to explain what I was doing. Even on a green light, people stopped and gave money. And although the traffic was backed up as far as I could see, all the way to the top of the hill and beyond the curve, nobody complained. Nobody honked a horn. I was astonished.

The entire time I was in Boston, our team captain educated and uplifted the young members. Another of Werner's lessons left a deep impression on me and continues to benefit me to this day. He said, "Volunteer for *everything*. Any time volunteers are called for, raise your hand and step forward. You don't know what you're capable of. You don't know what God expects or wants of you. But when you volunteer, you give God the option of choosing you. If you're not the right person for the task, don't worry. God won't choose you. But give Heavenly Father that chance. Always volunteer."

On a number of important occasions, his words would echo in my mind and push me to volunteer, even when I was reluctant or unsure. The first occasion came very soon.

I had been in the church only a few months when members from far and near gathered at our Belvedere Estate in Tarrytown, New York. We were there to celebrate a church holiday. After lunch, the elder in charge of fundraising, Rev. Kamiyama, announced the creation of national mobile fundraising teams (MFTs). He explained the concept and the mission, and then asked for volunteers.

After a moment of hesitation, my captain's words echoed in my mind, "Volunteer for everything." Conflicting thoughts and emotions arose, but the words kept insisting: *There are no exceptions to 'everything.' Volunteer for everything.*

I raised my hand and stepped forward. A few voices rose in protest. "No! You're too young … only a few months in the church! You need more experience to be on MFT."

I stood firm. It was in God's hands now.

Rev. Kamiyama stepped over to evaluate me. *Is it true? Is she too young? Not tough enough?*

People say that he had spiritual vision, that he could look at a person and accurately judge his or her character. He looked steadily at me and I looked right back at him. After a few moments he smiled, took me by the elbow, and walked me to the center of that empty space on the lawn, a space into which only a few had stepped. God had chosen. Thus began an amazing nine months on MFT.

The Metal Factory

So many of the unforgettable moments of my life came from experiences I had while on the national MFT. One such moment came when our team was fundraising in an industrial area. I can still see the endless railroad tracks and the freight cars parked behind factories and plants. I had difficulty with this kind of terrain, and *this* day was particularly difficult. I had not been connecting with people; I was repeatedly getting kicked out of places before I had a chance to get started; and I was disheartened. I needed to stop and pray.

I walked over to the parking lot of the next building. Finding an inconspicuous spot by a curb, I sat and rested my bucket of flowers. I leaned into the bucket and, with my face hidden among the flowers, I prayed in tears. I was there for a while, sharing with God my difficulty and repenting for wanting to give up so easily. When I had nothing more to say, I pulled myself together. It was time to give it another try.

Finding an entrance at the rear of the building, I walked in. It was a humongous plant, glaringly bright, hot, and noisy. Red-hot molten metal was being poured into vats or molds. Sparks were flying. I approached each person at his or her station, each representing one of the various stages of production.

Angels must have gathered around me, leading me on as I wandered the dangerous maze. I smiled and hugged my bucket. It was so noisy that shouting was futile. I abandoned speech and resorted to gestures. Walking up to each worker, I waved a few lovely carnations, wafting floral fragrance toward his or her nose for a complimentary sniff. I held up fingers to suggest a donation, depending on the size of the bouquet.

The workers melted. They were kindhearted and donated with a smile. No one was negative; no one kicked me out. A young woman wandering around with a bucket of flowers must have seemed a surreal apparition.

After completing my tour of the main floor, my flower bucket was nearly empty. Regardless, when I noticed the stairs leading up to the thick panoramic windows that were probably the plant managers' offices, I climbed the stairs to ask for donations. In response, I was advised of the hazards to which I was exposed and was swiftly escorted out the front door.

But no matter. This exhilarating experience had felt like a miracle. It had washed away the frustrations and difficulties

I had previously encountered in that challenging industrial area. More significantly, it seemed like a response to my tearful prayer, the outpouring of my heart to God. During that memorable episode, I had felt God's watchful loving presence and His uplifting encouragement.

Angels

On another occasion, I felt the presence and assistance of angels. It was a winter night. Snow and sleet had been steadily falling. Our team was on a highway, heading to a new destination. Because of the snow and the late hour, traffic was light.

The driver was making his way carefully along the highway, which was fast filling with snow. I happened to look up just as we hit a slick spot. The van slid sideways, toward the median, which turned out to be a fairly deep gully. As we approached the edge in slow motion, I began to pray, "Heavenly Father, if it's Your will, then please take me. But if it's not, then please help us."

The van reached the edge of the road. Then down the bank it went. We tumbled and rolled, tumbled and rolled several times before coming to a stop. In the process, I was fully alert.

As we tumbled down the slope, we passengers were like clothes in a dryer, going 'round and 'round. But rather than feeling pain, rather than feeling battered as heads, limbs, and bodies bounced helplessly against the vehicle's walls and windows, seats, floor, and ceiling, I distinctly felt enveloped and cushioned by what felt like thick layers of cotton balls. I felt the tumbling, but it was cushiony and soft.

Huh?

In response to my unspoken question, I became aware that the fluffy soft cottony cushioning, the thick, soft padding was in fact angels, the bodies of angels. They were holding us in their arms, surrounding us as we tumbled round and round. The angels were taking all the hits.

The van was damaged. It had been packed with crates of glass snifter candles that got tossed around with the people. But amazingly there was only one minor injury: Emily had a small cut on her cheek, probably from the broken window next to her seat.

When we came to our senses, we looked around.

"Are you alright?"

"Is everyone okay?"

We straightened ourselves upright. Bright red drops of blood, symbols of what *might* have been, trickled down Emily's pale cheek.

The van had come to rest on its side. The silent snow continued to fall.

Soon we heard voices. From the side of the van that faced up toward the snowy night sky, a door opened. The anxious face of a state trooper peered in … and then gradually relaxed. He was glad to see us alive and in one piece. Based on the condition and location of the van, he had expected to find us in far worse shape.

One by one we were pulled out by the trooper and other kind drivers who had stopped to help. We thanked them … as well as those *other* angels who had been there watching over us.

Angry Woman

In the parking lot of an average-sized shopping center, I was having an average day on MFT. It was neither too hot nor too cold, too sunny nor too cloudy. There was nothing out of the ordinary. People were making contributions at an average rate.

A woman was placing her just-purchased groceries into the trunk of her car.

"Hello! My name's Pauline. How are you?"

"I'm just fine," said the woman, glancing at me as she continued to pack her trunk.

"I'm with the Unification Church. Would you like to make a donation to support our work, in exchange for some flowers?"

"No! I would not!"

"If you prefer, you could give a few coins. Anything at all would help."

"No. I do *not* want to give a few coins. Go away! And religion doesn't help anyone!"

"I'm sorry. Why do you say that?"

"You shouldn't even be here! I should report you to the police. You're bothering people with your religion. And God doesn't give a damn! Where is God? Huh? What kind of God lets people suffer? Tell me that! There is no God!"

I shook my head and managed to say only, "I'm sorry."

The woman jumped into her car and slammed the door. She glared at me as she backed up. Her face was an angry shade of red and she was nearly choking.

I was stunned but waved goodbye as she mashed the gas pedal and peeled out. Then I walked around in a daze, contemplating what had just happened. After a while, I got back to fundraising.

Suddenly a speeding car drove up and jerked to a stop. The window rolled down and it was … that woman. She was wild-eyed and open-mouthed. I braced myself.

Panting, she managed to say, "Thank God! I found you!"

She caught her breath and continued, "I've been driving around this parking lot looking *everywhere* for you. I want to apologize. I'm sorry. I should not have spoken to you that way."

"Oh, thank you, ma'am. I appreciate that." I truly did.

She got out of her car. "Here! Please take this. For your church. I'm sure you're doing good work." She handed me several bills.

And then she poured out her heart. "I shouldn't have talked to you that way. But … you see … I just lost my daughter. She had cancer. I can't understand how God could do that. I'm so angry. I'm angry at God. But I shouldn't take it out on you. I'm sorry. I hope you can forgive me."

All I could say was, "I'm so sorry … I'm sorry about your daughter…."

Tears streamed down her face. She continued to tell me about her daughter, the cancer, the pain and suffering, her death, and God. Here was a mother sharing her broken heart with a stranger in a parking lot.

Was I any comfort to her? I would like to think so, even if all I did was listen.

Evidence of Things Unseen

Home, home on the range
Where the deer and the antelope play,
Where seldom is heard a discouraging word
And the skies are not cloudy all day.

—Brewster M. Higley

"Home on the Range" was one of my father's favorite songs. He sang or hummed it often, perhaps even as a lullaby. One day I found myself humming it as I was fundraising in the parking lot of a shopping center somewhere in middle America. The day was fairly normal, except that I couldn't stop singing that song—or thinking about my dad.

Later that day, as had scores of others, a middle-aged man walked across the lot, approaching one of the stores. Automatically, as I had done scores of times before, I greeted him with, "Hello. I'm Pauline Pilote. I'm with the—"

"Wait a minute!" he interrupted. "*What's* your name?" he asked, leaning over and peering at my ID badge.

I repeated, slowly, and pointed to the name on my badge.

He looked intently into my face. "Pilote!" he exclaimed. "I know someone named Pilote. Where are you from?"

"Maine."

His eyebrows rose. "*Where* in Maine?"

"Lewiston."

He was smiling now. "Are you any relation to *Guy* Pilote?"

Now it was my turn to be surprised. "Yes! He's my father."

Once again, I felt my father's presence.

"You're Guy's daughter!" He shook his head as he absorbed the news. "I was on the police force with him in Lewiston. How is he?"

He doesn't know, I thought. "Oh! I'm sorry … he died … about ten years ago."

The man's smile faded. He took a step back and leaned against a car. I felt I should comfort him. "I'm sorry. You didn't know?"

"No. I've been out of touch. I'm so sorry." Then, trying to be delicate, he asked, "Did he die … in the line of duty?"

"No. He had a heart attack."

My dad's friend was visibly moved. After a few moments, he asked about how my mother and siblings were

doing. Then he explained to me how he had left Lewiston …
and was now serving on the police force of *this* town.

Dad's police buddy had obviously respected my father
and had enjoyed working with him. For a long time, he stood
with me in the parking lot, telling stories about people and
events they had experienced together.

I didn't know much about my father's life outside of our
home. In front of the children, he had seldom spoken about
his work or about the world he experienced as a law
enforcement officer. Thus, it was a treasured gift for me to
meet this man, someone who had worked so closely with my
dad all those years ago.

Long into the rest of that day and evening, I reflected
upon this remarkable coincidence. In fact, I was confident
that it had not been a coincidence. I had felt my father's
presence with me the entire day. In the end, I hoped that he
had enjoyed the encounter between his daughter and his old
friend at least as much as we had.

The Watch

It's accurate to say that our MFT (mobile fundraising team) members loved our captain and he loved us. Like a big brother, Jeff cared for each one of us. He made sure that we had daily spiritual enrichment through prayer, scripture reading, and mini-sermons. When the winter got cold and the snow too deep for shoes, he took us shopping for warm clothing and boots. On special occasions, we shared cozy meals together at a diner or restaurant.

Equally important, Jeff fostered the creation of loving bonds among the team members. We became like close-knit members of a family and, as with most families, living and working in close proximity day in and day out meant that any degree of disharmony would become immediately apparent. Thus, when Jeff sensed discord brewing between Cheri and me, he came up with a plan.

Prior to meeting the Unification Church, Jeff had been a Cistercian monk. Spiritually attuned and extremely sensitive and perceptive, he may have been aware of a transcendent as well as a psychological component to the growing friction between Cheri and me.

I had had a healthy amount of respect for Cheri from the moment we met, many months prior, at my first *Divine Principle* workshop. She was an exemplary human being with many excellent qualities, and I certainly understood why she had been chosen to be our team mother. Nevertheless, I was finding myself at odds, more and more frequently, with her way of doing things.

Jeff came up with a plan. His idea was to create a more harmonious and loving bond of sisterhood between Cheri and me … by having us trade watches.

Are you kidding? was my initial — though unspoken — reaction. *This is mine! And it's expensive!*

In fact, only God and I knew the significance of that watch. It had been presented to me under very special circumstances. As my eighth-grade graduation from Holy Family School had approached, a local jeweler donated two beautiful gold-bracelet Bulova watches to be awarded to the top two students, one in English, the other in math. As it turned out, I was the student in English.

When the watch was bestowed upon me, I felt loved — profoundly loved — not by any particular person or being, but rather by the cosmos. Although I couldn't verbalize it back then, the watch came to represent God's love for me. That beautiful gift, so graciously bequeathed, was like manna from heaven.

It was for this reason, and not because of any monetary value, that the Bulova had come to be my most cherished possession. And now Jeff was asking me to exchange it for Cheri's Timex.

I prayed about it. I knew that Jeff was coming from a monastic tradition. I sensed that I was being asked to embrace a small act of asceticism, a form of spiritual discipline. And I realized that the arrangement was temporary — and for my own benefit as well as Cheri's. In the end, I embraced the idea. In my heart, I made the offering.

Jeff's plan worked. Every day, Cheri wore my expensive gold Bulova and I wore her humble Timex with the leather strap. From time to time throughout the day I'd glance at Cheri's Timex, and then I couldn't help but think of her and pray or meditate about our disagreements. In time, I came to see her through more loving and compassionate eyes. My heart melted and I grew to love and respect her once again. We arrived at a place of peace and harmony.

The watch exchange was not intended to be permanent. One day, however, Cheri accidentally left the Bulova in a public restroom. Ironically, she had taken it off so as not to damage it while washing her hands. When she went back for the watch, it was gone! She was so deeply remorseful about losing it that I couldn't help but forgive her.

What did I learn? With a sincere heart, I had placed the watch on the altar and gone to make up with my sister. In the process, I had discovered that my relationship with Cheri meant more to me than any watch. I discovered that living in harmony with and loving other people was more rewarding and more satisfying than any status or material possession. I learned that it was possible to forgive and to love one's enemy. And above all else, I realized that I no longer needed an object, no matter how precious, as a reminder of God's love for me.

Sunday Mornings with True Parents

I was on that initial MFT for about six months before the team was split up.[52] Over that short period of time, we had become a close-knit family.

Our captain, the former Cistercian monk, had been an especially kind, devoted, and perceptive brother. On his team, I grew and matured in my faith. My relationship with God developed into a more personal and intimate one. I came to better understand myself, my strengths and weaknesses. And I learned to get along with—and love—all types of people.

After being on Jeff's team, the one sure thing about my subsequent MFT experience was that everything was in flux. The changes kept me on my toes, adjusting to new people and new places.

For about a month, I was in the Chicago area. Then in April of 1975 I went to Ohio where, at first, I had trouble

---

[52] Jeff, our captain, was promoted to a different position, and the members of his team were sent to join other teams across the country.

connecting with the new team captain. Over the next few months, however, he grew on me. In my parting journal entry, I wrote: "I've come to appreciate Bob: deep heart, very quiet person, much love. So patient … like Heavenly Father Himself."

In late May, my situation changed yet again. Along with several other well-seasoned fundraisers, I was sent to a new mission, working with a ginseng tea company. As a large cohort of trainees, we gathered in New York to form an Il Hwa Korean Ginseng sales team.

We were educated about the ginseng root and the history of its therapeutic benefits. We learned about processing techniques and the quality of the Il Hwa products. We studied management and sales strategies. Once we began reaching out to customers, I was assigned to a suburban neighborhood in Queens, New York.

One of the benefits of being in and around the New York area back then was that we could go to Belvedere on Sunday mornings to hear our beloved True Father speak. [53] Driving up in the early morning, we would arrive in time for hymns and prayer just prior to the 5:00 a.m. Pledge Service with True Parents.

Reciting the *Pledge* is how Unificationists remind themselves to keep God at the center of their lives. The words of the Pledge have changed slightly over the years, but its

---

[53] Unificationists refer to Reverend and Mrs. Moon as the "True Parents" or "True Father" and "True Mother."

essence has stayed the same: we take responsibility to create God's kingdom on earth by striving to embody true love for God and for our families, our nations, and the world.[54] Admittedly not easy tasks, these are nevertheless worthy goals.

Pledge Service would be followed by more hymns and prayer, and then by the moment when Father would step to the microphone and, in his native Korean language, offer a long and usually tearful prayer that had many of us weeping along with him. Then he would pause and look at each one of us, or so it seemed to me, before beginning to speak.

Most memorable to me was his voice, his raspy voice and how, whenever he paused for the translation, he would look at us intently, sometimes smiling, sometimes serious. He seemed capable of looking at a person and sensing what he or she was feeling or thinking. Sometimes the content of his talk would touch upon those issues and provide answers to a person's intimate prayers or concerns.

As he increased in passion and in the intimacy of his sharing about God's suffering heart and God's love for humanity, Father's voice, nearly weeping, would rise in pitch but decrease in volume until sometimes he was speaking barely above a whisper and the translator would have to bend closer to hear him, or even to ask him to repeat himself.

---

[54] "Family Pledge," Family Federation for World Peace and Unification.

Father's sermons, the intimate sharing of his heart, created a profound sense of oneness with the audience. He was the teacher who energetically and dynamically instructed, standing for countless hours, pouring out his love, devotion, and passion for God and for humanity. He shared everything, shedding tears and sweat as well as wisdom, never losing an opportunity to raise us up so that we would all the more quickly transform ourselves to become the kind of children who can bring comfort to the heart of God, our Heavenly Parent. Father Moon was able to draw us into his own intimacy with God so that we too felt like God's own beloved children.

That was the key, the ultimate purpose: above all else, Father taught us to love God. His entire life was a living sacrifice for the sake of God and God's children, all of humanity. For Sun Myung Moon, there was no day or night, no mealtime, no vacation time. Foremost in his mind was the accomplishment of God's will to reach His children and to help them assume responsibility to restore themselves to their original, unfallen, divine selves.

On those special Sunday mornings, although I was most grateful for Father's heartfelt sermons, I was also glad to see True Mother and some of their children who were there with us. I was intrigued by Mother Moon. As she sat quietly near the stage, attentive to Father's words, I would occasionally look up to discover her gazing at me. Our eyes would meet and she would smile. At such moments, her smile seemed to encapsulate unconditional love and affirmation. She would observe others in the audience as well, sometimes smiling but at times radiating empathy and compassion even to the point of tears.

Although Mother was not center stage back then, she was nevertheless a substantial presence, willing to be brought to the foreground to illustrate a point in Father's speech, to brighten the mood, or for any other reason. On Holy Days and at other special gatherings, we came to expect that Father would ask her to sing for us. She would graciously comply, and Father would challenge her composure by singing along out of tune or off beat or in some other comical way designed to trip her up. She would nevertheless gracefully complete the song, all the while acknowledging Father's humorous sabotage. To me, her willingness to stand and sing or testify manifested an admirable composure.

Over the years, I have discovered that True Mother is exceptionally generous. Based on testimonies from many women in the church (some of whom happened to be wearing Mother's clothing or jewelry at the time I spoke with them) I discovered that she has a habit of giving away her best possessions. In fact, Mother Moon believes that "A world where everyone gives their best things to others is a world of joy."[55] Such thinking reveals a mother's heart. Now, although the gifts and blessings that True Parents bestow upon the

---

[55] Hak Ja Han Moon, *Mother of Peace*, 279.

world are much more significant, their loving hearts remain the same.

Exciting and novel as this period in New York was for me, it was too short. After a few months, the ginseng sales team was pared down and many of us were sent to other missions. I went back to MFT, at first to a team in the Southwest. We started out in Texas, moved westward, and eventually ended up in California.

A few months later, I joined a new team, this time in Georgia. I was there for only two weeks when, in early September, I found myself heading out to the newly-created Unification Theological Seminary to join the first class of seminarians.

Unification Theological Seminary

My nine months on MFT had been a period of growth. In 1975, a new opportunity arose when Reverend Moon founded the Unification Theological Seminary (UTS) and every interested college graduate in the movement was invited to apply. I was so excited. I had been wishing for more time to study the Bible. It would be a great blessing for me to be among those seminarians.

I applied, and in September I found myself seated beneath the stained-glass windows of the seminary chapel where our founder stood addressing the fifty or so incoming students of that first class. He counseled us to invest wholeheartedly into learning as much as we could, and to hold our faculty, which had been assembled from a wide variety of religious backgrounds, in the highest esteem.

The professors were a mix of liberals and conservatives, religiously as well as politically. Their academic backgrounds were equally diverse. A Catholic priest taught psychology and counseling classes. A Polish Jesuit offered a number of philosophy courses. One professor of biblical studies was an ordained minister of the Dutch Reformed tradition, while a professor of church history was a Texan minister from the Churches of Christ. By the second year, a Jewish rabbi (professor of Old Testament studies), a church history professor from the Greek Orthodox tradition, and a Confucian scholar joined the faculty.

At that time, the only female professor on the faculty was a Korean theologian, a Unificationist who taught classes in world religions. Gradually, the diversity of the UTS faculty was expanded to include more women and an even greater multiplicity of nationalities, races, and religious backgrounds.

Among the initial fifty students, a multitude of nationalities was represented. In addition to the Americans were Austrian, Dutch, French, German, Indian, Italian, and Japanese students coming from a variety of religious backgrounds including Christian, Hindu, Jewish, and Zoroastrian.

The initial two-year program was for a master's certificate in religious education. Because the seminary had just begun the process of accreditation, it would be unable to bestow actual degrees until a few years later. But to me that didn't matter; it was the education itself that I appreciated.

It was enriching and gratifying to be able to locate my personal faith within the broader historical-theological-religious context. I relished the classes in the history of the Christian church, systematic theology, philosophy, world religions, and biblical studies. In the process, I learned to appreciate my intellectual side. And for the first time in my life, I read almost the entire Bible.

Before attending seminary, I had known little about the world's religions other than Judaism and Christianity. It was important to understand them, however, because one of the goals of the Unification movement is to create a foundation for lasting peace by bringing harmony amongst the world's faiths.

For this reason, the course on "World Religions" was a core requirement. The class was taught in ways that engendered respect and appreciation for the diverse religious traditions and for the cultures in which they have evolved.

If it is the same God who reaches out to different peoples at different times, within and through their own unique contexts, then it's reasonable to expect that although perceptions, insights, and discernments may vary, there will nevertheless be universal truths and other elements in common among the world's religions. And that is what I found.[56]

The senior and junior classes of the seminary lived and worked closely together for two years, which fostered the development of meaningful and lasting bonds. And although

---

[56] Rev. Moon later sponsored the creation of *World Scripture* (ed. Andrew Wilson), a text that compares the teachings of world religions and reveals their common elements.

we were students, we were not at all in an ivory tower; we were not isolated from the rest of the Unification movement.

For example, along with other Unificationists, we helped bring audiences to Father Moon's public speaking events at Yankee Stadium and Washington Monument in 1976. Our outreach activities in connection with these events involved working with Christian ministers and with clergy of other faiths. These activities were integrated into our academic program.

As students, we also participated in academic conferences, for example those hosted by the International Conference on the Unity of the Sciences (ICUS) and the Professors World Peace Academy (PWPA). In February 1977, a wealth of opportunities for interreligious and theological dialogue was initiated. One of our professors of systematic theology invited a number of his former students, who were now theologians at universities across America and Canada, to come visit UTS to dialogue with a small group of seminarians. I was fortunate to be among them.

The topic of discussion that weekend was, in fact, the Unification Church and Unification theology, which had been rising to prominence as a subject worthy of consideration. That first dialogue generated so much enthusiasm among the theologians that it led to additional seminars and eventually to the creation of the New Ecumenical Research Association (New ERA), which soon began hosting international theological conferences.[57] Over the years, many Unificationist students, myself included, had the privilege of participating in several of those conferences.

In addition to the academic growth, the spiritual enlightenment and development, and the enduring friendships that were nurtured during those early years at the Unification Theological Seminary, there were many unforgettable, life-changing hours spent with Father Moon. The seminary was so much on his heart and mind that he came frequently to visit the campus. He gave inspirational talks. We engaged with him and asked questions. Those visits were occasions for heart-to-heart experiences that deepened our faith in God as well as in our own abilities.

Some of our most unforgettable moments with Father, which marked the beginning of a seminary tradition, were connected with fishing in the Hudson River. For decades, he had investigated ways to develop fish-harvesting and fish-processing so as to expand food resources for the hungry, especially in less-developed countries. Thus, it was no surprise that, from time to time, our attention would turn to fishing.

I believe that Father may also have been motivated to come upriver to fish with us so as to unite us through a common effort. He wanted us to challenge ourselves, to discover and push beyond our personal limitations, and to learn the value of teamwork. Finally, our fishing ventures

---

[57] "New ERA Ecumenical Conferences."

encouraged us to enjoy nature, in particular the beauty of the Hudson River Valley.

Making Nets

One memorable event with True Father was our first fishing expedition on the Hudson River. It was the spring of my final year and I was turning twenty-five. Someone had come up with the idea of using nets to fish the lagoon on the seminary side of the river.

In an initial phase of the project, we seminarians did some manual digging to expand a natural pond on the property. The idea was that the pond might hold, perhaps for fish farming, the carp that we hoped to catch. We toiled side by side, laughing and getting to know one another on deeper levels. This activity went a long way toward fostering the sense of family and supportive community that had already been developing amongst us. The digging was also a healthy diversion, a fresh-air physical activity that broke up the routine of long hours of lecture and study.

In the second phase, Father showed us how to customize the nets to achieve our purpose. As I worked on the net, my thoughts turned to Jesus' disciples, some of whom had been fishermen. Here we were, making nets and preparing to fish side by side with the man whom Jesus had personally called. How precious that was!

Two of our classmates, Matsuzaki and Daikon, had previously fished with Father on the ocean. For this new project, they had been assigned to purchase nets and other materials that we'd modify according to a design that Father had in mind. The plan included sewing nets together to make one gigantically long net.[58]

The idea was that at high tide, when fish were in the lagoon, students would block the inlet by walking the long net into the lagoon, in a semicircle. Then we would advance toward shore, making the semicircle smaller and smaller. Theoretically, the fish would be trapped in the net as we pulled it to shore.

In the net-making phase, we were outdoors behind the main seminary building on a grassy expanse surrounded by ancient trees. Beyond that were more fields, meadows, forest, and the river. It was spring. Everything was fresh, green, and vibrant. A bright sun warmed the cool air.

Father was there to personally supervise the activities. As a group of students watched, he demonstrated how to stitch together two nets. Then the students took over the task, and Father walked around, observing and giving instructions to other groups. In my section, we were sewing lead weights onto the bottom edge of the net. This was to ensure that the

---

[58] For another perspective that incorporates multiple episodes, see Peemoeller, *Bodyguard for Christ*, 141-145.

foot of the net would sink down, skim along the floor of the lagoon, and leave no gap for fish to escape.

It was characteristic of True Father to be oblivious as to whether it was day or night. Once he began working on something, he didn't stop. I don't recall what time we started making the net, but when darkness fell, lights were set up on the field so that we could see what we were doing. We continued sewing ... and sewing ... and sewing.

Someone brought sandwiches. I grew weary. At times my eyes closed, netting shuttle in hand. Coffee arrived. We kept working.

From time to time a seminarian would pause to gaze at the beautiful night sky. Along the Hudson River, so deep in the New York countryside, the Milky Way is an awesome sight. As bookworms and academicians with heavy workloads, few of us spent time stargazing on a regular basis.

Eventually Homer's rosy-fingered dawn appeared. As the sun met the horizon, I got my second wind and decided to stay on to finish the job. At that moment, from just behind me, a Korean elder called out, "Okay! Father says go take a rest. Everybody, get some sleep."

I turned around. True Father was standing there, in the doorway. Perhaps he had been there all along. Perhaps he had been observing, listening to our conversations throughout the night. We had talked about so many things, mundane as well as profound.

Fishing with Father

At last comes the day of the fishing expedition, the trial run, our first day of fishing with the nets.

We rise before dawn and put on our gear. We've planned it all in advance: we'll wear layers of clothing to conserve body heat. Although winter is behind us, the Hudson Valley in upstate New York is still cool. On this pre-dawn morning, there's a chill in the air and we know the water will be cold.

Some are donning boots—yes, boots for the lagoon—to protect against the prickly burrs that lie on the muddy bottom. We secure our socks and pants with rubber bands or twine to keep the burrs from reaching our skin.

In the dim light of early morning, we walk down the winding trail toward the river and lagoon. Single file or in pairs, mostly in silence, we help each other as we trip over tree roots, our hearts racing in anticipation.

Arriving at the railroad tracks, we turn right and walk carefully along the stone embankment built for the train to travel between the river and lagoon. A bridge spans the inlet, allowing the current to flow beneath.

In the dawning light, as we approach the lagoon we see that Father is already there. He waits for us on the opposite side, together with Matsuzaki and Daikon. One stands on the shore with Father, while the other is in a small rowboat.

We make our way along the embankment still slippery with dew and wet algae. A few students are there already, equipped with the nets.

True Father, watching our arrival, sees at a distance a commuter train approach. He shouts and gestures for us to beware, to move away from the tracks. Those up front hear him first, and in a domino effect, they turn to those behind and shout and gesture for them to get off the tracks.

The train advances. It flies by—a blur—a *whoosh*—a blast of wind. The ground shudders. Then all is quiet.

I look at Father as he stands in the distance. I feel his love for us. We resume our trek.

The plan is that we'll line up along the embankment, our backs to the river, facing the lagoon. Each person will hold a section of net and, together in one line, we'll step down the embankment and into the water.

As we hold the net upright, we'll walk forward to encircle the lagoon, all the while ensuring that the weighted bottom of the net stays flush with the muddy riverbed—so that no fish escape. We'll walk our semicircle forward, together with any fish trapped within, toward the opposite shore, as we gather the net and make the semicircle smaller and smaller. In this way, the fish will be edged toward shore,

127

concentrated in the ever-shrinking portion of net and, in the end, gathered up and pulled onto shore. At least that's the plan.

We take our positions and pick up our section of net. I stare at the dark water and brace myself, knowing that at any moment I'll have to step forward into *the abyss*. I fight to squelch my fears, irrational as well as rational.

I fight against my fear of dark, murky water in which I imagine unseen and unknown dangers. I fight against my thoughts of the river soaking my clothes and numbing me. More than anything else, I fight a primal fear of snakes and snake-like things like eels, which I know are plentiful here in this river.

I cannot stop obsessing about the eels. During our pre-dawn preparations, while others were concerned about sealing their clothing against prickly burrs, I was concerned about sealing mine against eels. I didn't want them slithering up my pant legs, touching my skin.

Now, as I stand on the embankment and look down on the surface of the cold dark water, I'm filled with dread. To calm my nerves, I joke about my phobias with a kind brother who stands nearby. He reassures me and I'm comforted.

Only now do I notice that the brothers are being especially solicitous toward their sister seminarians. I notice that the women have been evenly spaced among the men, in case we need assistance. The Japanese women in particular are vulnerable, their short stature virtually guaranteeing that they'll have to swim in some places with their portion of the net. Tall men are positioned on either side of them. There's another disadvantaged group here as well: the leanest of the seminarians. With little insulation, no fat to burn, they'll be vulnerable to the cold.

At last, after the dim light of early morning, the sun rises. The signal comes and we step forward. Down into the lagoon we go, careful to keep our footing on the slippery rocks of the embankment. We descend into the cold embrace of the river. We gasp, then force our lungs to inhale.

That's when I sense the familiar. *I've done this before … in the ocean off the coast of Maine … with my siblings. I can do this!*

From the stifled moans and the trembling, contorted faces of my classmates, I realize that others aren't as fortunate. Nevertheless, we press on.

Up to our chins in water, we step cautiously along the slimy, muddy bottom, gently pushing the net forward with our feet as well as our hands. We advance slowly, half-floating and half-walking, in sync with our companions. We encourage one another. We joke.

And with every step, we sink into the mud. Each step pulls at our shoes or boots, sometimes sucking them off completely. If a shoe is not retrieved, a person will have to walk on the prickly burrs that lie on the murky, muddy bottom. That's why, whenever the hungry mud tries to eat someone's shoe, we stop and wait for him or her to put it back on.

People around me discover their limitations. Some of the smaller women are overwhelmed and their neighbors support them until the boat arrives to carry them ashore. An ultra-lean brother braves the ordeal until he too succumbs and is taken ashore.

Despite their tribulations, the line of seminarians holding the net inches forward. I lose track of time.

Eventually, I notice that those who entered the water first, those at the head and tail of the net, will be among the first to step ashore because the net is being gathered in from both ends. I take courage, seeing that my time to step from the lagoon approaches.

Suddenly my attention turns to a wiggling around my ankles.

Oh! No! Are fish escaping under the net?

Using my feet, I try to push the bottom of the net down farther, but in the murky water I can't see what's happening. I don't know whether I'm being effective.

The wiggling around my ankles continues. Now it moves upward, along my leg.

Please … No…!

Something is swimming up my pant leg.

Please! Let it be a fish! A fish … not an eel!

My rubber band must have snapped. I'm no longer alone. We … that cold creature and I … advance together toward the shore, skins touching.

Scarcely able to breath, but not wanting to abandon my section of net, I keep walking. Then a humorous thought enters my mind. It distracts me and I cling to it like a mantra. *Once on shore, I'll be able to say that I caught a fish.*

By now my feet and legs are numb. In a meditative state, I'm intrigued that insensate legs still follow the dictates of the mind; they continue to move in the right direction, bringing me ever closer to shore.

From time to time I wonder whether the creature in my pant leg is still there or whether it has escaped—or even died. That last thought makes me sad. It's then I realize that I've already offered that fish to God as part of our catch.

I awaken from my reverie, only a few persons away from shore. True Father stands there, on the rocky bank at the edge of the lagoon, observing the scene. At his side, a few seminarians gather in the net and help people take their final shaky steps onto the rocks and up the bank to level ground.

As I approach, I notice that no fish have been caught. The gathered portion of net is barren and there's not much of it left in the water. It's unlikely there will be a catch today. Then I remember: my fish.

My good friend Tony stands beside Father, helping people step onto the rocks and up the bank. *Dear brother Tony! If I can reveal my secret cargo to anyone, it's you!*

He takes my arm to steady me ashore. As I step onto the rocks, aware that Father is watching, I whisper to Tony and point to my leg. He laughs and bends over. Lifting the hem of my pants, he gives a few exploratory shakes. A fish, very much alive, falls into his waiting hands.

"Look, Father!" he exclaims with his characteristically beaming smile. "We caught a fish!" And with outstretched arms he presents the fish to Father.

A huge campfire awaits us. Several of True Parents' older children have come down to the river. They tenderly wrap each student in a warm blanket and guide us closer to the fire. They place cups of steaming cocoa into our shaking hands. Soon, in small clusters and as we regain our strength, we thank our benefactors and head back up the trail toward the dorms, toward warmth and dry clothing.

Such are my memories of this indisputably unique fishing expedition. It was the first and—to the best of my knowledge—the only such undertaking. In terms of tangible results, it was an experiment that failed. Nevertheless, it had been rich in lessons of all sorts, and it led to the refinement and improvement of fishing the lagoon.

In subsequent episodes, a net was placed at high tide across the entrance to the inlet. Only a few people were needed for this process, which could be accomplished in a matter of minutes. Hours later, at low tide, more students would assemble and, in bright sunshine, wade into the shallow water to scoop up the stranded fish by hand. Photographs and testimonies of these expeditions, a tradition that continued for many years, attest to much merriment and good cheer.[59]

For me, the first fishing expedition was a cherished opportunity to spend time with True Father, every moment of which was unforgettable. Additionally, our venture into the lagoon confirmed our ability to exercise spiritual or mental dominion over our bodies; it was a way of discovering and pushing against our limitations—as well as of finding our strengths. Finally, the undertaking demonstrated the power of teamwork, of trusting and supporting one another.

I believe it is fair to say that, for every person there, the first fishing expedition was a rite of passage. Moreover, it foreshadowed what lay ahead: in just a few weeks we were to graduate into the wider world, where we would confront a myriad of hurdles and challenges. In hindsight, our fishing expedition recalled another historic moment of fishing, after which the participants were transformed into fishers of men. That was to be our destiny as well.

---

[59] For other perspectives on fishing expeditions at UTS, see Jones, *A Heart Made Whole*, 158-162 and Peemoeller, *Bodyguard for Christ*, 141-144.

"Brother, Can You Spare a Dime?"

My two years at UTS were idyllic in many ways: academic, spiritual, and interpersonal. Seminary life was a time of growth, and although at times it was challenging, for the most part I was not far outside of my comfort zone. I relished the academic work, and my participation in church campaigns, like those promoting the Yankee Stadium and Washington Monument rallies and speaking events, was well organized and sensibly focused on reaching out to churches and clergy. After graduation, however, the predictability of seminary life vanished and I was challenged by a series of rapidly changing assignments.

Because our opinions and academic contributions at conferences and in interfaith work had been appreciated, the seminarians had been treated with respect and even deference. As a result, some of us had come to expect that after graduation we would be assigned to positions based on our educational preparation. But instead of this I was surprised when I—along with many other graduates—was sent out to join a fundraising team.

In hindsight, I see the wisdom of this approach. We had received our seminary educations on full scholarships supported by the fundraising efforts of our brothers and sisters in the church. It was only fair that we repay the debt, or at least that we pay it forward. That explains why, on a bright sunny morning in the summer of 1977, I found myself sitting in a van beside the unpretentious and down-to-earth members of a mobile fundraising team, somewhere in a hot climate of the United States.

I was on a team headed by Bob, my former team captain from back in Ohio just prior to my enrollment at the seminary. Fortunately, I had departed the team with a great deal of respect for him. I appreciated his humility and the depth and kindness of his heart. So here I was again, back with Bob.

But I was not the same person. Two short years earlier, I had been an enthusiastic fundraiser managing all sorts of challenges. Back then, it was those challenges that had made each day rich in intangible rewards of personal growth and a deepening relationship with God. Back then, interacting with scores or even hundreds of people each day had enriched me and deepened my heart.

After I entered the seminary, however, my focus changed. Brimming with intellectual curiosity, I immersed myself in my studies. I excelled in my classes and, over the course of the two-year program in religious education, I developed a sense of how I might contribute to God's providence by using my new-found knowledge and talents.

In this respect, I was not unique. Father had often shared with us his high expectations regarding our future contributions to the movement, which had sacrificed to invest in our education. Seminarians had already begun to represent the Unification movement at conferences attended by world-class academicians and leaders.

That's why, on my first day back on MFT, I was disoriented. The way I had learned to think and communicate as a seminarian had not prepared me to return to a mission of fundraising. To my astonishment, I found myself virtually incapable of approaching people to ask for donations. I can laugh about it now, but on that first day I was paralyzed.

I had been sent to Bob's team, somewhere in the Midwest. Or maybe it was the South. But what did it matter *where* I was? It was somewhere hot, and I was simply there, stunned and confused. On that first day, I was dropped off in the parking lot of a shopping center, carrying a crate of scented candles.

After an initial prayer that proved to be inadequate—because I had no clue about the dragon I was about to face—I entered the arena. But I had donned the wrong armor.

I had forgotten that the essence of fundraising, in the Unification tradition at least, is not about raising money. It is about training oneself to see people—and to interact with them—from God's perspective, with God's eyes and heart. It is about learning to love people from a divine point of view, and about humbling oneself to be able to hear God's voice speaking through that of the other person. What better preparation for ministry?

Thus, it is not strategy, technique, or even the spoken word that's important. Fundraising is about developing one's inner mind and one's attitude of heart and love for the people. It's about self-discipline as well as achieving goals. That's what fundraising in the Unification movement is about. And I had forgotten.

Instead, I was poised to go through the motions. I approached a few people and forced words out of my mouth. But something was missing; I couldn't connect. After a while I just stood there, watching shoppers come and go. I looked at the people, anticipated interacting with them, but was unable to move. The thought of asking a stranger for a donation was daunting.

Clearly, this was not good. I needed to assess the situation. Perhaps I could pray or think my way out of the impasse.

At the edge of the blistering parking lot was a shady spot that called to me. A steep grassy bank led down to a stream. The bank was one side of a gulley, green and tree-covered on both slopes. Shady trees grew everywhere, up and down along the banks. A soft breeze refreshed me. Birds twittered peacefully. I sat on the grass and closed my eyes, grateful to inhale the healing verdure.

For a long time, I prayed and meditated. Tears poured from my eyes as I tried to work my way out of the quagmire, delaying the moment when I'd have to get back on my feet and give it another try. To God I repented sincerely.

From time to time, I'd turn around to survey the hot parking lot behind me. Then the beautiful green oasis would sigh and pull me back into the shelter of its shade. Although I had a strong sense of duty and responsibility, the right choice was daunting. This kind of fundraising seemed out of sync with the intellectual I had become.

I waited for the day to end, waited for the team captain to pick me up. When the van arrived, I got in without saying a word.

The other members did what every team does toward the end of the day. They talked and shared their experiences as they counted up and handed in the money. We ate a quick dinner, probably from McDonald's. Then we drove to the next phase, that inevitable final phase of the fundraising day: we were going *blitzing*.

Blitzing is a form of fundraising done mostly at night after the parking lots have emptied. The team captain drops people off at bars, restaurants, and other nightlife spots. Once the entire team is deployed, the captain circles back to pick up the first ones out, only to drop them off at a new location. The process continues until all available territory has been covered.

I was dreading the moment when Bob would say that it was my turn. Every time he stopped the van, I cringed. He must have sensed this.

In the past, as an enthusiastic fundraiser, I would have been among the first to jump out of the van on a blitz. But on that night, I was the last.

I had anticipated all the things Bob might say to encourage and inspire me to go out, things that team captains typically say to motivate their members, like "Do it for God!" or "Do it for True Parents!" Those two imperatives generally succeed at encouraging even the most reluctant person to at least give it a try. After all, who can say "no" to God?

Bob stopped the van. Slowly, he turned in his seat. He looked at me. In his gentle voice he said, "OK. This is your spot."

I shook my head. "I can't. I can't do it."

Instead of impassioned exhortations, the ones that I was prepared to resist, Bob said simply, "Please. Do it for *me*."

That was so unexpected. His humble request disarmed me. I did not have the heart to refuse. I stepped out of the van.

Out on the sidewalk, to God I simply said, "I'm sorry. I have nothing left to give. This is just my body going."

I opened the door. I walked in.

The bar was full. My body walked up to the person nearest the door. I set my box down on the counter and looked at the man. I said nothing. I didn't even smile.

Then something remarkable happened. He reached for his wallet and asked "How much?" I managed to suggest a donation. He gave me a bill. I gave him a candle. I moved over to the next person and the same thing happened. Again, and again.

The customers must have been talking. There must have been noise or music, but I was oblivious. It was like I was viewing it from a distance. Stupefied, I watched as God and the spiritual world did all the work. All I had to do was *be* there, walk around, carry my box. I was astonished.

Somehow, I got around to every person in that bar. Every person cheerfully gave a donation. Within minutes, my box of candles was empty. I had barely spoken a word except to suggest a donation and to utter a "thank you."

In the process, by the grace of God, I had been resuscitated. I had been reminded that God was right there beside me. I learned that I did not have to do or say anything spectacular or brilliant in order to succeed. I simply had to *be there* on behalf of heaven and to make whatever effort I was capable of. God would do the rest.

Tuna!

That first remarkable day of fundraising after my seminary graduation turned out to be my reintroduction into a world of heart in which simplicity, humility, and kindness are virtues. Not only that, but the awesome power of those qualities was ably demonstrated by my team captain, that soft-spoken, mild-mannered, humble and unassuming Bob.

Aside from that dramatic day of initiation, I don't remember much about the months that followed. One by one, the seminarians were called away from their interim assignments and given leadership positions.

In the fall or winter of 1977, Father assigned me to lead the church in Louisiana. I joined the handful of members in Baton Rouge who were evangelizing the campus of Louisiana State University. After a few months, we relocated to our church building in New Orleans.

Unification Church centers across the United States were self-sufficient. With whatever resources we had, whether many members or just a few, we engaged in evangelism, education, public relations, and fundraising—on college campuses, in urban downtown areas, and door-to-door in local neighborhoods.

Local church centers pooled their resources to bring guests to regional workshops at which the *Divine Principle* was taught. Our aim was to teach the *Principle* to open-minded people, young and old, wherever we could find them.

On a monthly basis, it was the custom for the state leaders to meet with Father Moon. We would share testimonies, give reports, and receive guidance and inspiration. Over the course of one of those meetings, convened in July of 1978 at Morning Garden,[60] Father took us out on the ocean.

I was among the lucky ones to be on Father's boat. So that I wouldn't get seasick, I kept my eyes fixed on the horizon, but some on the boat became so ill that they hung over the rail, vomiting nonstop. A small motorboat had to come out (we were pretty far out) to carry them back to shore.

I can still picture Jaime, a fellow seminary graduate who was leading the mission in West Virginia, as she knelt on the deck and cheerfully cut bait for chumming.[61] Others bustled about cutting bait, baiting hooks, and securing carefully

---

[60] "Morning Garden" was the name of our church-owned property in Gloucester, Massachusetts.

[61] Chumming is the act of tossing cut up pieces of bait into the water so as to attract the intended fish.

coiled lines and ropes into baskets.[62] Some kept watch over the other boats in the distance.

What was I doing? I remember only inhaling the ocean spray and feeling it on my face, in my eyes, my mouth, my hair. That world of sea and sky engulfed me and I embraced it in return. I was cherishing the ocean, the partly sunny sky, the far-away horizon, the planet.

Oh, God! This … is … so … beautiful. Thank you! Thank you so much!

Of course, I was also hoping that we'd catch a tuna. Occasionally I'd turn to look at Father as he sat or stood at his perch at the front of the boat. Calm and clearly comfortable in his role as captain and fisherman, he was keenly attentive to the still, deep ocean and to the bustling state leaders. From time to time he gave directions to us or to his crew. He guided the helmsman and, when he felt we had reached the right spot, he signaled him to stop and cut the engines.

The other boats in the fleet followed suit. They stopped, maintaining a good distance from one another. This was a well-regulated, well-practiced enterprise. Father and the members of the crew had spent days, months, and even years learning the ropes, not only here in the Atlantic but also in

---

[62] A variety of lines, ropes, and colored buoys were used to ensure tensile strength as well as to indicate depth and distance of the hooked fish. For detailed specifications, see Peemoeller, *Bodyguard for Christ*, 94, 97-98.

the Pacific Ocean off the coasts of Korea and Alaska. Some of our members had become proficient fishermen.

From all sides of the boat we put baited hooks and lines out into the blue-grey ocean. We chummed. We kept a silent vigil, watching and waiting for a fish to bite. But not just any fish: we were on the hunt for Atlantic Bluefin tuna.

As we waited for our fish, we admired God's creation. We prayed and meditated. A spirit of harmony encompassed the boat.

At the center of it all was True Father, who loved the ocean. Back then, he practically lived on the ocean, in part to meditate on ways of solving the world's problems, in part to fish. For him, fishing was a spiritual as well as a practical activity. The two purposes coalesced, as when our fleets caught krill and small fish for processing into dried fish powder to feed people in impoverished nations.

Father's interest in Bluefin tuna had begun to be actualized in July 1975, when he and his crew went out to sea every day for twenty days straight. They left before dawn, at 4:00 in the morning, and didn't return until 6:00 or later in the evening. Eager to learn from the local fishermen, they carefully observed what the other boats were doing and, once back on shore, they listened as veteran fishermen spoke of their methods.[63]

In a process of trial and error, Father and his crew adjusted the materials and techniques they were using. After

[63] Peemoeller, 93-95.

twenty days, they had caught nothing, but their skills had improved. They were getting more strikes per day. Nevertheless, for a number of reasons including the snapping of fishing lines, the fish had been getting away. That's why it was significant that, on the twenty-first day, the first tuna was caught.[64]

After that, Father continued to experiment and to adjust his methods. Eventually, he

> developed his own special technique. First, he put seven-strand stainless steel wire on the reels, and that's how the first tuna were caught. He changed eventually to hand lines…. After Father perfected the skill of tuna fishing, the gear, and the skill of the crew, it became standard operation. [65]

Those hand lines were already in use by the time, in July of 1978, we state leaders were assembled in Gloucester for our memorable day of fishing. By then, the name Sun Myung Moon was well-known among the fishermen of that part of the north Atlantic.

How much time passed as we chummed, checked and rechecked the lines, prayed, and spoke in hushed voices? For a very long time the sea and all upon it was still.

And then … a strike! A tuna on the line! A shout went up as one of the carefully wound ropes swiftly unfurled into

---

[64] Peemoeller, 93-95.
[65] Peemoeller, 97-98.

the sea. Attached to that line, and last to fly from the boat, was an unsinkable float, a neon-bright buoy.

"Pull in the lines! Hurry!" A boat chasing a tuna needs space to maneuver.

Alerted, the other boats, even those not part of our fleet, retrieved their lines and steered clear. To and fro above the waves we followed the bouncing buoy as the fish pulled from beneath, trying to escape to the depths. We sailed forward, following our fish to the left and the right.

Then, abruptly, the buoy stopped. The line went slack. It floated in random squiggles on the water.

"All stop! Stop!"

"Where is he?"

Silence.

We strained to see into the dark abyss. Then the buoy … began to move … toward the boat. The fish had doubled back, desperate to escape his tether.

"Under the boat!"

"Astern! Behind us!"

Was he beneath the boat? If so, the line might get tangled in the propellers. Using grappling hooks, the crew expertly maneuvered the line and its buoy clear of the ship.

And, once again, the line became taut as the tethered tuna swam away. We turned and followed. All the while, crew and passengers of the other boats watched and cheered.

At last, the buoy stopped. This time, someone hooked the rope and began to pull it in. But the fish fought back. It was a long contest, a fight between one giant tuna and one crew member after another, each side single-mindedly determined to overpower its mighty opponent. Whoever came up with the trademark "Chicken of the Sea" must have been a suit-and-tie kind of guy who never grappled with a giant tuna.

Over time, the fish tired. When he'd stop to rest, we'd pull him in closer. Between rests, he resumed his fight. But at last, it was over. I saw him now, a silver giant on his side, one sad eye looking up at me from the water. He was an eight-hundred-forty pounder.

God Chooses My Spouse

In April of 1979, after approximately one year in Louisiana, I was transferred to the church in Jackson, Mississippi. Life changed even more dramatically when, a few weeks later, news came regarding an event that had been greatly anticipated: the matching and engagement of couples. Eligible candidates were invited to gather at the World Mission Center in New York City. By that time, I was twenty-seven years old.

According to Unification theology, God's blessing of marriage is a key component in the process of restoring humanity to God's original ideal. The *Divine Principle* demonstrates that salvation is not an individual matter but is, rather, a family matter. Just as God cannot be happy existing alone in "heaven," so too an individual cannot feel joy in the absence of his or her loved ones.

A prerequisite of happiness, therefore, is loving, harmonious bonds and relationships. Humans need to feel loved and valued, and they need to give love to others as well. That is the definition of being truly human.

Finally, learning true love—love that is genuine and altruistic—begins in childhood, in a healthy family. The family is meant to be the school of love.

For these reasons, God's plan for the restoration or salvation of humanity necessarily involves the restoration of the divinely ordained family. The Blessing of Marriage in the Unification movement is a step in the process of restoring individuals and families.

Following their own Holy Marriage Blessing in 1960, the True Parents began matching and blessing couples according to the guidance of God. Thus, when I became eligible to be engaged in 1979, I trusted that God, through Father Moon, would choose my future spouse.

Nevertheless, I'm the kind of person who seeks confirmation and assurance regarding matters of importance. Mercifully, God has always provided me with the patient, loving support that I need. Thus, when it came to being matched and blessed in marriage, divine confirmation was especially welcome. In fact, God prepared me in advance to know His choice for my spouse.

This happened while I was a student at the Unification Theological Seminary. Although I had grown confident of my intellectual abilities, I nevertheless remained respectful toward the wisdom of elders in the faith. When conversations turned to upcoming matchings or blessings, elders would at times share testimonies demonstrating the importance of remaining open to Heaven's suggestion for a partner. They shared stories about people who had brought grief upon themselves when, believing that they had received a revelation about a particular person as their future spouse, they were less than enthusiastic when True Father suggested a different person as a potential match. Such testimonies demonstrated that *apparent* revelations could be misleading ... and therefore should be taken with a grain of salt.

As it turned out, I unexpectedly found myself in that type of situation. While still a seminarian, I had a vivid dream in which I was bustling about a house that I gradually came to recognize as being my own home. In the living room on a green recliner sat a man reading a newspaper. Gradually, I became aware that the man in the recliner was my husband. After I realized *that*, I recognized him: a fellow seminarian. Then I awoke.

Predictably, one of my first thoughts was of those unfortunate people who had been misled by similar dreams or revelations. My first line of defense, then, was to share this dream with an elder.

I talked about the dream and about my concerns with Alice, an elder sister among our small group of women seminarians. I also spoke with the dean of students, who was also a woman. They both agreed that it would be wise for me to limit future interactions with this classmate, and that I should regard the significance of the dream with a healthy dose of skepticism. And so, I did.

After graduating from the seminary, I was in the habit of praying for several of my former classmates. In the spring of 1979, as I prayed for the person who had sat in the recliner in my dream, I felt God's own heart of compassion and love for him, and I began to cry. As I continued with my tearful prayer, I had a sudden, overpowering sensation. My inner soul or heart, God's heart, and the heart of this other person all melded together—as though we had bonded into a single heart, a single entity. The experience was overwhelming.

This must have been an act of God, I concluded. It had certainly been something beyond my control. But what did it mean? Did it mean that my earlier dream of this person had been prophetic, after all?

Not long after this, the True Parents invited eligible candidates to New York for a matching. Inside the Grand Ballroom of the New Yorker Hotel, which was the matching venue, I was especially prayerful. Although some candidates were looking around at potential matches, my own thoughts were turned inward. I was praying that I would wholeheartedly accept whomever Father might suggest for me. At one point, when the person from my dream came to mind, I wondered whether he had received news of this event … and whether he was present. Still, I affirmed to God that I would accept whomever He would choose for me.

After a sincere prayer, Father began by speaking about the significance—and the challenges—of international and interracial marriages. Then he asked for volunteers. After he matched some international couples, he asked for those who felt called to embrace an interracial marriage to come to the front of the room.

Should I volunteer? Given my lifelong concerns about racial harmony and my desire to help mend race relations, was this an opportunity for me to walk that path through an interracial marriage? Was I a suitable candidate?

Father was carefully observing each volunteer as he or she stepped to the front of the room. I was vacillating, still undecided, when the words of brother Werner, my first team captain, came to mind. "Volunteer for everything. Let God decide."

I stood up and began walking toward the front of the room. Seeing me approach, Father stepped forward as though to intercept me. Like a cowboy cutting a stray calf from the wrong herd, he waved his arm in a gesture for me to go back. "Too intellectual!" he said.

I had offered myself wholeheartedly. God had not chosen me. I was relieved. In my heart, those presentiments about my future spouse still carried weight.

I rejoined the seminarians and alumni at the rear of the room. When Father had finished matching the interracial couples, he strode to the back of the ballroom. Standing in the midst of the seminarians, he asked here and there a few questions.

Most of the time my head was bowed in thought or prayer, but when I heard Father's voice near me, I looked up.

He was pointing to me … and then pointing back to … that person from my dream!

My eyes opened wide, first in amazement, and then in relief. At last I knew. My dream, a few years back, and the more recent spiritual experience regarding my future spouse had indeed been from God. Now I could be assured that this was God's will.

The match-making process included time for private discussion and for a confirmation (or rejection) of each proposed match. Prospective couples gathered on the balcony to discuss personal matters like their hopes and dreams, potential for compatibility, and similar issues. My future spouse and I proceeded to the balcony.

As I have already related, he was someone I knew fairly well, someone whom I had admired during our two years as students at the seminary. On his part, however, I was not the type of woman he had been expecting: glamorous and sophisticated.

For a number of reasons, our discussion was rather one-sided. While he proceeded to inform me of the various perceived obstacles to the relationship, including a difference in age, I simply smiled and nodded. Without intending to, it may have seemed that I was dismissing his misgivings as being unimportant. But the reality was that, because I had already recognized the match as being part of God's plan, there was nothing he could say that would dissuade me. Moreover, being rather introverted, I could not conceive, under the circumstances, of sharing my perspective with him. Since he had no way of knowing the back story, he interpreted my acquiescence as a sign that I was in love with him.

After the matching and the engagement ceremony that followed it, people returned to their respective missions and ministries throughout the country and the world. For the most part, the newly engaged couples would get to know one another from a distance, by phone and by mail. The actual blessing of marriages would come later.

Religious Studies and Slavic Languages

I returned to Jackson to resume my church mission. Over the next several months my fiancé and I, who had been classmates, became better acquainted. And as the months flew by, there was even more for us to look forward to.

For one thing, I was overjoyed to have been approved to pursue a doctoral degree, supported by an educational grant from the Unification movement. It was late August when I left Jackson for Union Seminary in New York City.[66] I was doubly excited about the move because, as it turned out, my fiancé was also in New York—as a graduate student at Fordham University.

Immersed once again in biblical studies, church history, and theology, I thoroughly enjoyed my classes. Thanks to my grounding in Unification theology, the insights I was able to contribute enriched and energized some thought-provoking class discussions. My academic papers, nuanced by the new

---

[66] Union Theological Seminary is a non-denominational Christian seminary that is progressive or liberal in its approach to theology and its advocacy of social justice.

perspectives that I was presenting, elicited lively responses—and marks of distinction—from my professors.

Thus engrossed in my academic life, months passed before I realized that I had been neglecting my spiritual life. When I put sincere prayer back into my routine, the situation improved dramatically.

In retrospect, it's ironic that in a seminary, where people are supposed to be learning about divinity and developing lives of piety, a person can so easily become distant from God. My experience reminded me that, as with any relationship, it takes effort and investment to cultivate a genuine relationship with God.

My idyllic academic life was eventually jolted by a number of unpleasant realities. Partly because of the Unification movement's opposition to Marxist communism and partly because of its groundbreaking theology, during the late 1970s and early '80s, persecution of the Unification Church accelerated. Although Union Seminary had admitted several members of our church into its divinity program, there was an undercurrent among some faculty, administrators, and students that "Moonies"[67] ought to be kept at arm's length.

At first I only suspected the prejudice, but in February of 1981 it became obvious. Unificationist students at Union co-sponsored, together with a Union professor, a campus

---

[67] "Moonies" is a derogatory term used by detractors of the Unification Church.

event at which a prominent theologian, Dr. Gabriel Vahanian, was the guest speaker. Although the event had been adequately promoted, the size of the audience was surprisingly disappointing. When the Union professor apologized to our famous guest, he gave as the reason for the limited turnout the fact that Unificationists had been the co-sponsors.

That was the first time I became aware that Union Seminary was populated, to a significant extent, by people who were intolerant of at least one faith tradition: mine. Within another two weeks I would personally experience a malicious side to that bias.

A few months earlier, in keeping with my hope of transferring into the Columbia University-Union Seminary joint Ph.D. program in religion, I had submitted my application. As I anxiously awaited acceptance into that program, a respected member of the faculty admitted to me that influential members of the seminary community held prejudicial attitudes toward my church. In spite of this revelation, I continued to hope that my excellent academic record would override the bias.

Sadly, within a few weeks, I received a letter of rejection. I was astonished. I had done well academically and had the support of several of my professors, some of whom were on the admissions committee. When I investigated, I discovered that the professors had been denied the opportunity to review my application because it had been removed from consideration by a dean who had unilaterally decided that I was not to be admitted.

I had to revise my academic plans. When my advisor learned that I was thinking of changing my field of study in order to remain in New York with my fiancé, he was saddened. He hoped that I would find a way to continue in religious studies. When he learned that I had also considered Emory University's graduate school of religion, he affirmed the excellence of the school and encouraged me to apply. I did.

At the same time, I applied to the graduate program in Slavic languages at Columbia University. I had taken courses in Russian language in college, and I had an enduring and keen interest in Russian history and religion.

Both universities accepted my application. Emory offered me a full scholarship. Religion was my primary field of interest, but I decided that it was important for me to stay in New York so that I could encourage and support my fiancé as he pursued his doctorate in philosophy. Thus, I entered Columbia University's program in Slavic languages.

Meanwhile, I had decided that I would continue with and simultaneously complete the Master of Divinity program at Union. Working on two master's degrees at the same time proved to be challenging, and I often wondered whether I had made the right decision.

"If This Be of God..."

M y academic and personal situation, although a bumpy path, represented a minor subplot in the context of a broader and more significant story. The big picture was that my church, the Unification movement as a whole, and Father Moon in particular were under attack from many sides.

By the late 1970s our church had been growing rapidly, especially among young adults. In contrast, other Christian denominations had been losing members. As a result, some churches felt threatened, and Father Moon and the Unification Church became lightning rods, targets of religious bigotry and persecution.

On top of that, our ongoing and effective opposition (in the form of "Victory Over Communism" lectures) to the aggressive expansion of Marxist communism, both in this country and abroad, meant that the Unification movement was being criticized and attacked from that side as well. Then there was that undercurrent of racial bias. How could an Asian preacher elicit rapid growth in the U.S. while other

Christian ministries were in decline? Failing to consider the merits of the *Divine Principle*, the critics irrationally concluded that Reverend Moon and his church must be brainwashing people. Thus the "Moonies," as we were scornfully referred to, had to be stopped. But of what crime could we be accused?

At first, we became targets of sensational news stories trying to convict us of wrongdoing in the court of public opinion. But the accusations were unfounded and would not stick.

Another opportunity to get rid of us arose in the form of "Koreagate," the name given to an attempt by some leaders of South Korea and the KCIA to influence the U.S. Congress to reverse President Nixon's plan to withdraw American troops from South Korea.[68] Although Father and Mother Moon were legal residents of the United States, our adversaries hoped to implicate them as KCIA agents and, in that way, forcefully deport them. Thus, in 1977 Donald Fraser launched the Subcommittee on International Organizations of the House Committee on International Relations (the "Fraser Committee") to investigate Reverend Moon. After more than a year of digging, the committee was unable to find any wrongdoing. There was no connection between the Unification movement and Koreagate.[69]

---

[68] "Koreagate."
[69] H.J.H. Moon, *Mother of Peace*, 146.

After this attempt to stifle our church failed, the IRS—which had begun its own investigations in 1975—continued with their efforts to find reason to prosecute. Three reviews by the Department of Justice Tax Division failed to find cause for prosecution. Finally, a grand jury decided to charge Reverend Moon with filing false tax returns and conspiracy.[70]

The case was complicated. It involved issues of church-state separation, tax laws regarding tax-exempt status, and the general custom of clergy to control church funds. For that reason—and because of prior negative publicity and the widespread persecution of our church—in the interest of getting a fair trial, Father Moon asked for a bench trial. The request was denied. Instead, he was forced to undergo a trial by jury.[71]

At the time the charges were brought, Father was in Korea. The prosecutors hoped he would do them a favor and simply stay there, thus permanently leaving the United States. They even "offered to drop the case in return for Moon surrendering his green card, which he chose not to do."[72] Instead, because he was innocent, Father Moon decided to return to the United States to fight the accusations and exonerate his reputation.

Thus, on the morning of April 1, 1982, Father's trial began. In New York City, the day began as any other day;

[70] *United States v. Moon*, 718 F. 2d 1210 (2nd Cir., 1983).
[71] H.J.H. Moon, *Mother of Peace*, 146-7.
[72] "United States v. Sun Myung Moon."

but just as the lead prosecutor began his opening arguments, a freak storm arose in and around the City.[73] Out of nowhere, an incredible wind exploded and raged.

I experienced it firsthand as I walked to my 10:35 AM class on the Columbia University campus. Then, as I sat in the classroom (room 716) atop Hamilton Hall, the raging winds grew to extraordinary proportions.

Days later, as I was reflecting on the events, I wrote in my journal:

> … the weather was so weird. The wind began to blow so furiously that one had to walk backward to protect one's face—and it had been mild and warm just a short while earlier. While I was in Composition class, the wind was howling and rattling the windows … I felt God's power…. Then I saw dark clouds cover the sky—until it was very dark—and I felt so deeply that it must have happened this way at Jesus' crucifixion.

> Later, I learned that people in the courthouse were freaking out as the courthouse windows rattled and the whole building shook. (Fact: some buildings in NYC were damaged that day.)

About six weeks later, on May 18, 1982, the jury declared Father Moon guilty. He was fined $25,000 and sentenced to eighteen months in federal prison, although the

---

[73] "April Blows in Like March" and "Rev. Moon Goes on Trial in City on Tax Charges."

Justice Department had estimated (in 1981) that the tax liability was just $7,300.[74]

It happened that, over the course of the trial, I was studying the book of *Acts*, a biblical record of the tribulations of the new religious sect that developed into Christianity. The Lucan narrative vividly reminded me of the parallel persecution of my own relatively new church. The Fraser Committee's investigation and the IRS audit, trial, and conviction had been the result of a chain of events propelled by the hate-filled bias of impassioned critics. Their zealous attempts to discredit a man of God who had committed no crime vividly reminded me of a similar situation in the first century, when Jesus' disciples and apostles were brought before a court. I could only wish that the politicians and accusers of our era had been mindful of the wisdom of Gamaliel, whose words still echo in my mind.

> But the high priest rose up, and all who were with him ... and filled with jealousy they arrested the apostles and put them in the public prison....
>
> Now when the high priest came, and those who were with him, they called together the council, all the senate of the people of Israel, ... [and] they set [the apostles] before the council. And the high priest questioned them, saying, "We strictly charged you not to teach in this name, yet here you have filled Jerusalem with your teaching and you intend to bring this man's blood upon

---

[74] H.J.H. Moon, *Mother of Peace*, 147-148, 157; Orrin Hatch, Letter.

us." But Peter and the apostles answered, "We must obey God rather than men...."

When they heard this, they were enraged and wanted to kill them. But a Pharisee in the council named Gamaliel, a teacher of the law held in honor by all the people, stood up and ... said to them, "Men of Israel, take care what you are about to do with these men.... in the present case I tell you, keep away from these men and let them alone, for if this plan or this undertaking is of man, it will fail; *but if it is of God, you will not be able to overthrow them. You might even be found opposing God!"* [75]

Because the persecution of Reverend Moon had been so blatant, a number of prominent American clergy recognized his innocence and publicly supported him. Among them were the Reverend Jerry Falwell, Sr., head of the Moral Majority and co-founder of Liberty University, and the Reverend Joseph Lowery, a veteran of the Civil Rights movement who was leading the Southern Christian Leadership Conference.[76] In all, at least forty religious and secular organizations and individuals joined in filing sixteen *amicus curiae* briefs in support of Reverend Moon, with one of them representing over forty million parishioners.[77] Some of the organizations included the "Center for Law and Religious Freedom, the American Civil Liberties Union, the

---

[75] *Acts* 5: 17-39. Emphasis mine.
[76] Curry, "Clerics Urge Pardon."
[77] Friend, "Moon's Financial Rise and Fall."

New York Civil Liberties Union, American Baptist Churches in the USA, the National Council of Churches, the National Black Catholic Clergy Caucus, the Southern Christian Leadership Conference, the National Conference of Black mayors, and the National Bar Association."[78]

Members of Congress also expressed concern that the trial and conviction of Reverend Moon might represent a violation of religious liberties. On June 26, 1984, a U.S. Senate Subcommittee on Constitutional Rights held hearings on Reverend Moon's tax case.[79] Among witnesses and supporters who testified or submitted documents testifying to their concerns about violations of religious freedom were ministers and leaders of numerous denominations and educational institutions.

After the hearings, the chairman of the subcommittee, Senator Orrin Hatch, concluded that

> We accused a newcomer to our shores of criminal and intentional wrongdoing for conduct commonly engaged in by a large percentage of our own religious leaders, namely, the holding of church funds in bank accounts in their own names. Catholic priests do it. Baptist ministers do it, and so did Sun Myung Moon.
>
> I do feel strongly, after my subcommittee has carefully and objectively reviewed this case from both sides, that injustice rather than justice has been served. The Moon case sends a strong signal that if one's views are

---

[78] "United States v. Sun Myung Moon."
[79] "Issues in Religious Liberty."

unpopular enough, this country will find a way not to tolerate, but to convict.[80]

Slowly, the tide began to turn. Gradually, the Unification Church came to be viewed as a legitimate part of the American religious landscape.

---

[80] Orrin Hatch, Letter.

The Blessing of Marriage

In spite of the drama and turmoil of the IRS investigation and trial, on July 1, 1982, the long-awaited day of our Holy Marriage Blessing arrived. Early that morning, my fiancé and I were among several graduate students and their betrothed who shared cabs downtown from the Upper West Side. The cabbies were visibly stunned—and ours even thought he was hallucinating—when they arrived downtown to see more than two thousand couples, brides in wedding gowns and grooms in dark suits, all standing on the sidewalks near Madison Square Garden, the venue for the ceremony.

Inside, the Garden was beautifully decorated top to bottom. Multicolored banners adorned every tier. Flags of every nation hung from the high ceilings and were displayed around the stage. Friends, family, and special guests filled six thousand seats along the sides of the stadium, eagerly awaiting the entrance of the couples who would occupy every remaining space: the entire floor and the tiers of seats at the back of the Garden.

To the tune of Mendelssohn's "Wedding March," the procession of brides and grooms ceremoniously entered from the front. We filed past wedding attendants who looked like white-robed angels. We ascended a carpeted platform on which stood the True Parents, also in white robes, who from either side sprinkled holy water upon the couples as we passed. From there, the impressive procession continued along the vast floor, which had been covered with a snow-white carpet.

Once the couples had reached their designated areas and seats, the ceremony began. Together in front of God and all of humanity we made our vows. We promised

1. to become a true man or woman who practices sexual purity and lives for the sake of others;

2. to become a true husband or wife who respects True Parents' example and establishes an eternal family that brings joy to God;

3. to become a parent who educates his or her children to follow the tradition of true love for the sake of the family and world;

4. to create an ideal family that contributes to world peace.[81]

We exchanged rings. There were prayers and congratulatory addresses.

After the ceremony, the day was ours. Couples posed for wedding photos, dined with friends and family and,

---

[81] "Blessing Ceremony."

especially if they were strangers to New York City, went sightseeing.

For a number of reasons, our families had not been able to attend, so two of our friends from Union Seminary had come to share the day with us. At a nearby restaurant, we enjoyed lunch and exchanged animated commentary on the impressive wedding. As students of religion, our discussion naturally turned to theological issues.

We spoke about the significance of various elements of the ceremony and about how the Holy Marriage Blessing invites God's blessing upon the couple and their union. We explained how the original misstep of the first human ancestors caused humanity to lose awareness of the divine nature of marriage and family, which is meant to function as an essential channel for God's love to flow into the world.

Because we are eternal beings, marriage is meant to be an eternal bonding rather than something that lasts for only an earthly lifespan. It is meant to be an everlasting covenant between one man and one woman, with God at the center of the union. Together as a unit, a couple is meant to embody God, reflecting God's dual characteristics of masculinity and femininity, joined into one harmonious whole.

That is the ideal. But a harmonious marriage, like a harmonious world, requires investment. It requires long-term commitment in the face of difficulties and in spite of changing circumstances. To maintain their union, a couple must be willing to grow in tandem—not as individuals but rather as a team. For some people, that is too great a challenge. Thus, when faced with the inevitable obstacles and difficulties, not all of those marriages were going to be successful.

Upstate Saga

Marriage was the first step in a life-long journey of adapting and finding ways to live harmoniously with one another. We were older than many new couples: thirty and thirty-nine respectively. On some level that meant that we should have been more mature; on another level, it meant that we may have been more set in our ways and less flexible in finding happy compromises regarding our differences.

To deepen and strengthen the love and respect in a relationship, a couple needs patience as well as faith. In our case, since I knew that our relationship had been ordained by God, I had the faith. To what extent my husband shared that faith was yet to be determined.

As our personal lives were radically transforming, my husband and I continued with our graduate studies. In May 1983, I completed the Master of Arts program in Slavic languages at Columbia University and began the next phase toward my doctorate. In the same month, I completed the Master of Divinity program at Union Theological Seminary.

Meanwhile, we were expecting our first child. So far, I had succeeded in keeping all the balls in the air. *How difficult could it be to add "mother" to the mix,* I thought naively, *when I have already managed to complete two academic programs simultaneously?*

In the spring of 1984, while Father and Mother were grieving the loss of their son, Father's judicial appeal was denied and he was sent to serve eighteen months in federal prison.[82] Nevertheless, from behind prison walls, Father continued his work.

It was while in prison at Danbury that he, together with Mother Moon, famously convinced Dr. Morton Kaplan, professor of political science at the University of Chicago and the chairperson of the upcoming 1985 Professors World Peace Academy conference, that the title and theme for that conference should be "The Fall of the Soviet Empire: Prospects for Transition to a Post-Soviet World."[83] Going against popular and political opinion as well as the combined wisdom of academia, the True Parents understood that the Soviet empire was going to fall soon after its seventieth year. Father's earlier prophetic declaration about communism was about to be fulfilled.

---

[82] On December 22, 1983, their seventeen-year-old son Heung Jin Moon was critically injured in an automobile accident and died eleven days later.

[83] Professors World Peace Academy, "The Fall of the Soviet Empire."

At this time, my husband and I were supporting the activities of the Collegiate Association for the Research of Principles (C.A.R.P.) on local college campuses. We were there in 1985 when our dear friend Lee Shapiro was touring campuses to show his documentary film, "Nicaragua Was Our Home," a film about the Marxist Sandinistas' mistreatment of the native Miskito population of Nicaragua.

Our daughter was a toddler. One of my most vivid memories of the Columbia campus event was the sight of our precious child joyfully handing out leaflets, ecstatic over students who graciously accepted them from her tiny hands, and equally chagrined over those who declined her kind offer.

Another unforgettable recollection is that of the Marxist agitators harassing us as we chatted with people on campus. Later, as the film was being shown, they stood up in the auditorium and tried to shout it down. They did the same when the filmmaker came to the podium to speak. Nothing was out of bounds in their attempts to conceal the crimes against humanity that had been committed for the sake of advancing communism.[84]

On a personal note, the cost of living in Manhattan became prohibitive. The time arrived when we needed

---

[84] Later, Lee Shapiro made several trips to Afghanistan to secretly document the Soviet military involvement there. In October of 1987 he and his soundman Jim Lindelof were ambushed and killed.

affordable childcare. Until then we had been taking turns at parenting, switching off when it was the other parent's turn to work or study. While that had been a precious opportunity to spend time with our daughter, strolling through parks and playgrounds or the zoo, or stopping to hear street musicians, I had to step up my academic pace to fulfill the requirements before the clock ran out.

Because we had both completed our coursework, there was no need for us to continue living in town or near the campus. From a financial perspective, relocation seemed a reasonable option.

We had connections with the Unification Theological Seminary in Barrytown. My husband was teaching a class there, making the round trip north by train once a week. The on-campus childcare would be available to us. Finally, since the cost of living Upstate was less than that of the City, it seemed like the right choice.

A few days before Thanksgiving of 1985 we loaded up a truck and drove north. It was only later that I would reflect on how the upheavals of my personal and family life were occurring at a time of upheaval in the world. Global transformation, including the disintegration and collapse of the Soviet Union, was occurring during that same time period, 1985-1991. It is worth noting that on that very same Thanksgiving Day of 1985, as I unpacked our moving boxes, the farsighted Professors World Peace Academy conference on "The Fall of the Soviet Empire: Prospects for Transition to a Post-Soviet World" was convening.

As it turned out, life upstate became more challenging. Although my husband continued teaching his class at UTS, he took a full-time position editing church publications back in New York City. That meant that he would spend the week in the City and take the train back home on weekends.

In addition to that, time was running out for me to complete my doctoral program. I had finished the required exams; all that was left was to write a dissertation. After the birth of our second child, however, juggling two children and a dissertation became more than I could manage. Even with the help of childcare, I was unable to finish on time. This was a failure I found difficult to digest.

Then our family finances worsened. For one thing, we lost the student health insurance that I'd had through the university. It was a difficult period for America in general. The nation was in a serious recession, interest rates were high and climbing, and the cost of housing kept rising. The time came when I had to choose between paying for housing or buying food.

Credit cards were a novelty back then, and supermarkets had not yet begun accepting them as payment. Fortunately, gas stations and stores like Kmart did. Although the interest rates were excessively high, eighteen percent or more, at Kmart I was able to buy on credit things like infant formula, baby food, and diapers, as well as peanut butter and popcorn. From the gas station convenience store, with my gas card I could buy milk, bread, and eggs. Once a week, at the supermarket I would pay cash for one package of meat and a few items like rice or potatoes and vegetables.

Every day, my daughter's school lunch box consisted of a peanut butter and jelly sandwich and a small juice box. At home, in addition to peanut butter and jelly sandwiches and popcorn, I ate whatever my daughter left on her plate.

When my husband came home on weekends, I would make a meal using the one package of meat I had purchased. That way, he wouldn't realize the extent of our poverty—although he was generally aware that our finances were tight. To cut costs, he slept in his office in Manhattan, which fortunately was equipped with a full bathroom. Nobody knew he was living there. We were too proud to let anyone know about our situation or to ask for help. It was our problem and we would solve it.

One day, a friend of ours dropped by unexpectedly. He had brought a package of popsicles for my little daughter, who was his own daughter's best friend. When he opened the freezer to secure the popsicles, he was surprised. The freezer was empty.

Before I could stop him or offer an explanation, he opened the fridge. There was virtually nothing there either, perhaps just some eggs and a carton of milk. He looked into the empty cupboards. I had to say something.

"We've been going through a rough time, but we'll be moving to D.C. soon." A solution was just around the corner, I assured him. My husband had just landed a job as an editor at a magazine.

Still, our friend insisted on giving me money. Then and there he opened his wallet and put a hundred dollars in my hand.

"Pay me back when you can," he said.

I was touched and grateful, although it was an embarrassing moment.

As our family was facing these and other challenges in the late 1980s, the world was undergoing its own pangs of transformation.

Communism Starts to Crumble

The theme of the imminent collapse of the Soviet Union, at that prescient and well-attended November 1985 Professors World Peace Academy conference, may have been a mere pebble causing only a ripple, but the avalanche was soon to follow. Because I was preoccupied with my own affairs, I had not been closely following the broader course of historical and providential events. That's why I was pleasantly surprised to see, on television, President Ronald Reagan standing at the Brandenburg Gate on June 12, 1987 and calling out, "Mr. Gorbachev, tear down this wall."

By that time, I had come to trust that Mikhail Gorbachev's attempts at reform were sincere. This meant that Ronald Reagan's expectations were more realistically hopeful than they could ever have been during the earlier, bleaker days of the Cold War.

I recently discovered the impressive role that Hyo Jin Moon and CARP played in this chapter of world history. The eldest son of Father and Mother Moon was president of the World Collegiate Association for the Research of

Principles (W-CARP). During the fourth World CARP Convention in August of 1987, he prayed at the Berlin Wall and made a declaration reminiscent of Ronald Reagan's.

From the start, Marxists had opposed the plan to hold the convention in West Berlin. Their agitation and propaganda had elicited negative articles from the press, and one after another the convention venues had canceled their contracts with CARP. Eventually a suitable venue was obtained, but left-wing radicals heckled the speakers, threw paint and stink bombs during the events, slashed tires, and set fire to vehicles.[85]

A march to the Wall drew over 2,000 participants from around the world. The procession included "coffins depicting the millions of deaths under communism…. This was the most international demonstration against the Wall ever held in Berlin since its erection in 1961."[86]

Hyo Jin Moon led the march and echoed President Reagan's call for President Gorbachev to tear down the Wall. In an eyewitness account, German CARP representative Claus Dubisz relates that

> Two hundred leftists were waiting for us …. on the western side of the wall, where West Berlin police cannot enter. As they were shouting, spitting, and throwing cans [of paint], we blocked them with our banners. The Blue Tuna Band inspired all participants to sing "Die Mauer

---

[85] Dubisz, "Fourth CARP Convention."

[86] Dubisz.

muss weg!" ("The wall must go!") The leftists tried to destroy our placards and started to hit our members....

...at the Wall ... Hyo Jin Nim took the stage and ... condemning the crimes of communism, he declared: "That's the difference between communism and Unification Church members: We truly mean to bring about a peaceful world. Not by threats, not by power, not by materialism, but only by the truth of God, only by the love of God.... Come on, let's go to the wall and pray!"

Rushing through the crowd, Hyo Jin Nim went directly to the Wall and prayed so deeply that everybody around him started to cry with him.

We felt this marked ... the real beginning of Father's route to Moscow.[87]

The bravery and persistence of Hyo Jin Moon and the CARP members who stood up against the might of world communism reminded me of Joshua and Caleb who, with their own small army, faithfully marched seven times around the walls of Jericho before the walls collapsed. CARP's protest at the Berlin Wall may have seemed a futile gesture, but within days, brave souls *on the East Berlin side* gathered and also demanded that the Wall come down. As Dubisz relates, "in the following days amazing things happened. For the first time since 1961, a demonstration was held in East Berlin to protest the Wall. Young people there were also shouting 'Die Mauer muss weg!'" [88]

---

[87] Dubisz.
[88] Dubisz.

It would take two more years before the German people would stand at that Wall—and atop it—and begin to literally chip it apart with their hands, piece by piece and block by block. To me, that seemed like a miracle.

Looking back on these events, I feel that it must have been the hand of God that caused that East German official, on November 9, 1989, to err as he publicized a new policy. The policy had been intended to merely ease some of the harsh emigration and travel restrictions. But at a press conference, party leader Gunter Schabowski made his astounding—and inaccurate—announcement that border crossings would be allowed *without restriction* and effective immediately.

The miscommunication was due to last-minute changes in a draft of the policy, as well as to the fact that Schabowski had not attended the Politburo meeting at which the new policy had been worked out. Unaware of the changes in the draft, he was handed a note outlining those changes—but only just prior to the press conference.[89]

The one-hour press conference was broadcast live on East German radio and television. Stunned reporters asked follow-up questions for clarification. The confused Mr. Schabowski searched for answers by reading from sections of the note. It certainly seemed that border crossings would be allowed ... without restriction ... effective immediately.

---

[89] "Fall of the Berlin Wall."

Other media outlets quickly rebroadcast the news. Within hours, thousands of East Germans carrying their belongings were lined up at the exit gates. Confused border guards made frantic calls to superiors, who had also heard the erroneous interpretation of the new policy. The guards opened the gates and allowed the mass exodus. Then they watched as West Berliners danced atop the Wall and started chipping it away.[90]

Once begun, the avalanche could not be stopped. On December 22, 1989, the Brandenburg Gate was officially opened to unrestricted travel in both directions. In June 1990, East Germans joined in dismantling the Wall and reconnecting the roads and train tracks that had, for the past twenty-eight years, ended at the Wall. By July there was no longer a border between East and West Germany. On October 3, 1990, German reunification was officially declared.[91, 92]

---

[90] "Fall of the Berlin Wall."

[91] "Fall of the Berlin Wall."

[92] None of this happened in a vacuum. Widespread protests demanding change were occurring in other Communist Bloc and Iron Curtain countries. Moreover, Communist China's massacre of thousands of its own citizens on June 4, 1989 may have made other communist nations reluctant to follow suit when their own citizenry rebelled. The time was ripe for change, time to acknowledge the failure of governments that had, in the name of building communist utopias, killed millions of their own citizens. Estimates vary, but it's fair to say that in Communist China from 1958 to 1962, 45 million people were killed. In the seventy years

It seemed a wondrous miracle that, in front of the world and my own astonished eyes, communism had begun to crumble.

---

between 1917 and 1987, the Communist Party of the Soviet Union killed *at least* 61 million (and possibly 126 million) of its own citizens.

Saints in the Underground

Amazing and wondrous as this was, human affairs and human history do not occur in a vacuum. Humanity is interconnected, and every action, no matter how seemingly trivial, has an impact. Like a tiny drop in the water, there is a ripple effect ... with consequences that are either beneficial or harmful.

For decades, brave souls around the world had been risking their lives to expose the repressive and inhumane nature of communist governments. Their sacrifice (sometimes mortal) had contributed toward loosening the grip of global communism.

Because I could speak Russian to some extent, I had sometimes imagined myself studying at a university in the Soviet Union. Travel to the USSR was restricted in the '70s and '80s, but I wondered whether, embedded there as a foreign student, I might help prepare the way for that long-anticipated "March on Moscow" that Father Moon was envisioning as a step in the plan to transform and heal the Soviet Union.

Of course, I had been chosen to do graduate studies in theology and I was doing that, but whenever I was reminded of my other desire, my heart would ache. That was another reason why, in 1981, I enrolled in a master's program in the Slavic Languages Department at Columbia University. Although I had no concrete plan for how I might help, it seemed like the right thing to do. My yearning to bring relief to the people of the Soviet Union was powerful.

One night, after a bout of soul-searching, I had a dream. I was on a jet flying to the Soviet Union.

When we landed, I had no idea what to do. The moment I set foot on Soviet soil, however, I began to weep, crushed by an acute awareness of the suffering of the millions of victims, living and dead, of communism. To them in prayer I expressed my sorrowful compassion for their plight. Paradoxically, I also shed tears of joy: *I'm here!*

When I pulled myself together and looked around, I noticed something odd. Among the people at the airport, two stood out. There was something unusual about them: their bright spirit contrasted with the dark heavy spirit of the other people. Even the way they moved was different. A special aura seemed to radiate from them. And although they were doing nothing out of the ordinary, simply conversing with people or with one another, they reminded me of Unification Church members.

I had to find out. Gradually I approached them. When I made eye contact, they returned my gaze with honest eyes and a smile. Aware of the need to be circumspect in a nation that prohibits free speech and religion, we exchanged vague pleasantries, only gradually alluding to more substantive issues. Finally, it became apparent that we were indeed brothers and sisters of the same church family and that the church, although underground, was healthy and growing. Once again I wept, this time in gratitude that our missionaries were already there, bringing life and hope to the people behind the Iron Curtain.

I awoke from the dream relieved and comforted. Although I was not at that time aware that we actually *had* missionaries in the USSR (this was a closely-guarded secret until after 1992), the dream nevertheless soothed me. Somehow, I felt that things were going to work out, and that the dream had been a gift from God.

It was many years later when I discovered that our missionaries had in fact been there, behind the Iron Curtain, at first individually and then, from about 1980, in a more organized fashion. As it happened, in the late 1960s a few members of the European Unification churches had bravely decided to enter the communist countries of Eastern Europe. They went as students, as guides and interpreters for tourist agencies, or as employees of companies doing business there. Their purpose, however, was to find people who would welcome and embrace the teachings of the *Divine Principle*.[93]

---

[93] Kwak, *Mission Butterfly*, 13-14.

Over the years, more of our members joined the underground efforts. By 1980, Unification missionaries were in the Soviet Union as well as in its satellite nations. Careful to evade the KGB and similar hazards, they found creative ways to secretly teach the *Principle* and to recruit new members.

Sadly, not all of these brave souls remained invisible. Many were arrested. Some were tortured. Several were sentenced to years in prison. Others died mysteriously or were executed.

The sacrifices of these code-named "butterfly missionaries," their commitment to bringing God's love and truth to the people living under communist repression and oppression, surely moved God's heart. Their heroic work was an altar of sacrifice, a spiritual foundation upon which the True Parents were able to build and which ultimately led to their own meetings with Mikhail Gorbachev and Kim Il Sung.

Mother Moon credits the sacrifice of the underground missionaries as having been fundamental to the peaceful end of communism:

> I must add that all this would never have happened were it not for the work of the "butterfly missionaries" of our movement from Europe. Called to this mission, they … entered the Soviet Union and Eastern Europe as underground representatives of True Parents. The fall of the Soviet Union was the climax of God's invisible plan for which these faithful people had set conditions at the risk of their lives. Through a complex interweaving of

events, each of them played a role in bringing about the dissolution of the Soviet Union and the shift toward democracy. Even today, they continue to pray and work for religious freedom and social progress for Russia in its path forward.[94]

Only after 1992 was the presence of our missionaries behind the Iron Curtain made public knowledge. Before then, "Operation Butterfly Mission" had been a carefully guarded secret.[95]

---

[94] H.J.H. Moon, *Mother of Peace*, 200.
[95] Kwak, *Mission Butterfly*.

Onward to Moscow

As Father had predicted would happen, the iron bonds of Communism had begun to unravel by the 1980s. God's providence was advancing.

Within the Soviet Union itself, dramatic changes had been taking place, unseen by the outside world. For one thing, seven decades of centralized planning had left the economy and the infrastructure in shambles. On top of that, the Soviet invasion of Afghanistan in 1979 had dragged on for a decade, and citizens of the USSR were fed up and ready for change. When Mikhail Gorbachev became president, he introduced radical changes that included *glasnost*, a policy of more open discussion, and *perestroika*, a multi-level restructuring to end central planning.

When I first heard of the changes being implemented by President Gorbachev, I could hardly believe it. I found myself alternating between joyful relief and a jaded skepticism. It seemed far too unreal, too incredible, coming on the heels of seventy years of heartless inhumanity and deception. It could easily have been just another ruse.

On the other hand, many factors had contributed to a growing disenchantment with Communism. As mentioned earlier, the bravery of outspoken dissidents had exposed the corruption, deceit, and violence at the core of communist governments. Dissidents like Alexander Solzhenitsyn (*Gulag Archipelago*) had smuggled reports, testimonies, and evidence out of the Soviet Union in order to get them published. These brave souls had laid bare the truth that gradually shattered the world's naïveté, thus slowing the spread of communism.

In Korea, Father and Mother Moon and many of their compatriots had endured the widespread suffering caused by the communist regime of Kim Il Sung. Having first-hand knowledge of the evils of communism and of its failure as a system of government, they too made significant contributions toward exposing and putting an end to it.

From as early as 1965, CARP and VOC activities worked to raise awareness, in many nations, about the errors of Marxist theory and practice.[96] Other organizations like the Association for the Unity of Latin America (AULA), the CAUSA Foundation, Professors World Peace Academy (PWPA), and the World Media Association (WMA) sponsored international conferences that addressed, among

---

[96] Collegiate Association for the Research of Principles (CARP) and Victory Over Communism (VOC).

other topics, the aggressive and inhumane nature of communist repression and expansion. The *Washington Times,* *Tiempos del Mundo* in Latin America, and *Ultimas Noticias* in Uruguay exposed the corruption and human rights violations of communist governments.[97]

From as early as July 1973, Father Moon had been speaking of the need to hold a religious rally in Moscow. His call for that "March on Moscow" had become an oft-repeated mantra and in 1976, following his speech at the Washington Monument, he again affirmed that we should meet in Moscow … in 1981. The fulfillment of that dream, however, had to be postponed.

Meanwhile, for a decade the World Media Association had been convening international media conferences and building relationships with journalists, including those from the Soviet Union. In the 1980s, WMA sponsored fact-finding tours to the USSR. As Mother Moon explained,

> At that time, my husband and I sponsored the World Media Association fact-finding tours, taking Western journalists to see firsthand the conditions in the Soviet Union and other communist states…. Besides taking the blinders off these journalists' eyes, the tours generated positive relations with Russian media. On that foundation, my husband and I decided to go to Moscow to meet President Mikhail Gorbachev.[98]

---

[97] President Reagan praised the *Washington Times* for standing up to communism. See H.J.H. Moon, *Mother of Peace,* 177.

[98] H.J.H. Moon, *Mother of Peace,* 194.

It was because of significant contributions like these, including the hosting of Soviet journalists at the *Washington Times* in Washington, D.C., and an International Religious Foundation (IRF) conference in Moscow in October 1989, that the World Media Association and Summit Council for World Peace were invited to hold their 1990 conferences in Moscow.[99] Journalists, heads of state, and former heads of state from around the world were among the attendees.

It was as the founders of those organizations that the most famous and outspoken anti-communists in the world, the Reverend Sun Myung Moon and his wife Hak Ja Han Moon traveled to Moscow in April of 1990. Not only were they welcomed, but they were invited to meet with the president. Over the course of those two conferences, Father and Mother Moon met with President Gorbachev in the Kremlin, even speaking privately with him in his office.

On that occasion, Father advised the president that "the success of the Soviet Union depends on whether you put God at the center or not.... Atheism will lead to nothing but self-destruction and disaster." Father also conveyed to Mr. Gorbachev that "the only way for the Soviet Union to survive was for Russia to continue [President Gorbachev's] economic and political reforms *and to allow freedom of religion.*"[100] Those

---

[99] H.J.H. Moon, 197.
[100] H.J.H. Moon, 198-199. Emphasis mine.

few days in Moscow were as effective a "March on Moscow" as any that I could have imagined.

Soon after this, in December 1990 and February 1991, the USSR began to allow scores of its leaders to come to the United States to attend seminars sponsored by various organizations of the Unification movement. In July and August of 1991, 380 students and faculty from across the Soviet Union came to study the *Divine Principle*.[101]

Based on the enthusiastic response of these participants, the Unification movement was then invited to come to the Soviet Union—and to other Communist Bloc nations—to teach the *Principle* and a character education curriculum to thousands of students, faculty, and government officials. Hundreds of Unification Church members volunteered to teach and staff these seminars, which continued briefly into 1992 after the USSR was dissolved. [102, 103]

---

[101] Seuk, "The Soviet Student ILC."

[102] Mickler, "Educating Soviet Leaders," 353-356; and Devine, "The First National D.P. Workshop," 357-361.

[103] The situation changed radically after the Moscow Patriarchate of the Russian Orthodox Church (ROC), feeling threatened by the influx of religious groups after Russia's liberation from communism, pushed for laws to restrict religious and educational activities of religious bodies *other than the ROC*. Such laws were swiftly passed in 1992, and the Unification movement was no longer allowed to teach *Divine Principle* or its character education curriculum. From that time, the curtailment of religious freedoms in Russia has progressively escalated. See

On the foundation of the Unification movement's significant and successful activities in the Soviet Union, in December of 1991 Father and Mother Moon were invited to North Korea to meet with Kim Il Sung, the very man who had tried several times to have Reverend Moon killed. It was a surprisingly warm meeting.

Later, Father Moon was informed that Chairman Kim had testified to his own son and heir, Kim Jong Il, that Reverend Moon was "a great man. I have met many people in my life, but none were like him. He has a broad scale of thinking, and he overflows with heart. I felt close to him…. After I die, if there are things to discuss pertaining to North-South relations, you must always seek the advice of [Reverend] Moon."[104]

To this day, organizations within the Unification movement, including the Universal Peace Federation, continue their efforts to peacefully unite the two Koreas.[105]

Lamoreaux & Flake, "The Russian Orthodox Church…" and Tony Devine, "The First National DP Workshop," 357-361.

[104] S.M. Moon, *Peace-Loving Global Citizen*, 262.

[105] Universal Peace Federation, https://www.upf.org/

Moving to Maryland

Prior to these mind-blowing and miraculous events, as the old world in its death-throws transitioned to greater freedom in Eastern Europe, my family and I over the same time period (1985–1991) struggled to keep our heads above water. We lived with hunger and the prospect of becoming homeless. Our marriage was suffering for a number of reasons including financial stress and the fact that my husband's job kept him out of town, away from the family, for the entire workweek.

As we struggled to survive, my bond with and compassion for the suffering and enslaved people of the Soviet Union endured. Despite the atrocities committed by their misguided nation, I still loved "Russia" and I continued to hope and pray for its eventual liberation and restoration into the family of God.

There came a day, however, when my hopeful idealism collided with the stone wall of reality that was the "Soviet Empire." Our dear brother Lee Shapiro had been traveling back and forth to Afghanistan, documenting the Soviet military presence there. On one of those trips, in October of 1987, he and his soundman Jim Lindelof were ambushed and killed, allegedly by Soviet troops (according to their mujahedeen escort).

When I first heard the rumors, I hoped they were untrue. At the time, I was at the library of the Unification Theological Seminary, so I walked over to the chapel and knelt on the stone floor. As I prayed, I sensed that Lee had in fact ascended to the spiritual world. To be honest, as I prayed begging for the rumors to be untrue and for God to protect him, I felt Lee standing by my shoulder and confirming that he had, in fact, been killed. He was calm about it, as though he had already reconciled himself to the situation.

Immediately, an avalanche of rage spewed from my heart. It smothered me and I choked on the unfamiliar feeling of furious hatred toward the USSR. Yes, they had unjustly taken the life of my brother, a man passionately dedicated to eradicating the suffering of God and of humanity, but for nearly my entire life I had embraced the people and culture of what had once been Russia. Now those conflicting emotions, the love for Russia and the raging hatred toward the Soviet Union, clashed violently within me. How could I reconcile such evil … with a heart of love?

In the end, I knew that I could not carry that poisonous hatred in my heart. As Lee himself must have done, I had to forgive them.

In spite of the difficulties, our family managed to hold on during those historic years until thankfully my husband landed a job as an editor at a monthly magazine in Washington, D.C. Our family relocated and there, with the help of friends and the ever-watchful divine benevolence, I was introduced to the president of the publication at the very moment when he was seeking an executive assistant. I was hired and virtually overnight my world was transformed from darkness to light. I had failed to achieve my academic goals, but life was moving forward. My family was no longer threatened by hunger and deprivation, and in the following year our third child was born.

Life normalized. We were able to manage private school and daycare for the children. We had medical insurance. Our children moved from a precarious existence into a relatively privileged and enriched one. It was a period of blessing, even later when private school became less affordable and they had to transfer into public school.

My husband and I juggled family and professional life as we tried to maintain a healthy balance. When my boss assumed responsibility for additional media organizations, I was invited to transfer over to the next office as his assistant. In this way, I moved from the magazine to a video production company and then to a daily newspaper.

It's fair to say that working for the dynamic president of these organizations meant that there was never a dull moment, and I matured professionally, personally, and spiritually. Nevertheless, after nine years I was ready for change, and it seemed that, once again, the stars were aligned: I discovered that I could easily become certified to enter the teaching profession. A critical shortage of teachers had prompted local Boards of Education to invest in recruiting and training qualified persons to transition from other careers into teaching.

For me, there were several advantages to this career change. First of all, teaching was a profession in which my creativity as well as my intelligence would be more fully utilized. Although well-aware that the education bureaucracy would dictate and micromanage on the basis of whatever political and academic dogma and jargon were then current, in the classroom at least I would have the liberty of planning and conducting instruction according to my own expertise, as long as I achieved the goals—and used some of the methods—imposed upon me from above.

Secondly, as a parent, my own children's schedules of abundant school holidays and vacation time—including winter break, spring break, and summer break—would become more manageable. I would automatically have the same vacation days as they.

Finally, although I would begin at a lower salary than that of my current job, I was guaranteed increases virtually every year. Moreover, a pension would be available to teachers after a minimum of ten years of service.

I went for it. After some initial training—and with a synchronized process of additional training and certification in place—I became an English teacher at a middle school. Four years later, feeling that my pedagogical skills and personality might be better suited to a more mature student population, I transferred to teaching high school students. It became obvious that I had made the right choice.

Meanwhile, one would think that with our financial situation so greatly improved, the stress on our marriage would have been alleviated. But that was not the case. Our marriage was a challenging enterprise and, for a marriage to succeed, both partners must commit to making it work.

Because God had already assured me of His choice for my husband, I had no doubt that we were meant to be together. I believed that everything would eventually work out. But gradually, over the next twenty-one years, our marriage would unravel and I would find myself among the divorced.

Nevertheless, I believe that an integral part of God's plan for us was the three wonderful children who were born. Their broad minds and big hearts testify to a deeply ingrained, altruistic purpose that guides their lives.

Our elder daughter, a lawyer, works to help refugees. Our son, with a heart to serve his country and help people in times of natural and man-made disasters, is in the Army National Guard. Our younger daughter has dedicated herself to a career in nursing and in caring for others. As adults, they travel their own unique paths and are not affiliated with the Unification movement.

Jesus Assures Me

Because our lives and finances had stabilized after our move to the D.C. metro area, I had time for volunteer activities like teaching Sunday school and helping with lay ministries. I supported the Women's Federation for World Peace (WFWP) and the interfaith activities of the American Clergy Leadership Conference (ACLC).[106]

Among its many endeavors, ACLC empowers religious leaders with tools and strategies for strengthening and uplifting their congregations. Given the modern-day erosion of moral values in our increasingly secularized societies and cultures, that need is critical. My contribution was to reach out to clergy and invite them to dialogue with their

---

[106] ACLC is "a coalition of clergy working to strengthen marriages, rebuild families, restore communities, and renew the nation and the world.... Clergy of the American Clergy Leadership Conference share the hope of leading all humankind into becoming One Family under God." ("Statement of Purpose")

counterparts in events like pastors' forums, interfaith prayer breakfasts, and interreligious conferences.

It was in 1936 that the young Sun Myung Moon was first called by Jesus to take up his ministry. He was asked to unify Christians in a fellowship based on mutual love of the Lord and on loving one's neighbor as oneself. To achieve that goal, in 1954 Reverend Moon founded the Holy Spirit Association for the Unification of World Christianity. Throughout his lifelong ministry, he has encouraged Christians to unite with one another and to work together. On such a foundation, Christianity will be able to reach out to the world's other religions and promote harmony among them as well.

"I know that what hurts God's heart more than anything else," says Mother Moon, who has embraced and continues Father's legacy, "are the religious conflicts that take place in His name. Without fail, we will end them."[107]

Peace on earth will not be possible until there is peace among the world's religions. To encourage that process, in the 1980s Father Moon invited seven thousand American Christian clergy, in a series of ecumenical groups, to visit Korea. It was based on their interactions and on the friendships that developed that the ACLC was born.

Later, in 2003 an ACLC delegation of several hundred Jews, Christians, and Muslims prayerfully walked the streets of Jerusalem chanting "Peace, Shalom, Salaam Aleichem."

---

[107] H.J.H. Moon, *Mother of Peace*, 100.

This interfaith group, including its Jewish participants, was invited into the holy places of the Al-Aqsa Mosque and the Dome of the Rock.[108]

My previous studies in theology, scripture, and world religions had created in me an affinity for interacting with clergy. Thus, I was grateful that my occasional work with the ACLC allowed me to develop enlightening and enriching relationships with a variety of churches and pastors. But there were some difficult experiences as well.

Several years ago, for example, I met a Baptist minister and, on a number of occasions, attended his church. I found him to be closed-minded, judgmental, and hate-filled, all of which, in my opinion, were incredibly un-Christ-like.

In one memorable sermon, he spewed forth a passionate condemnation of all Catholics, including the Pope himself. All Catholics were, quite simply, "going straight to hell." He actually said that.

Because of this one experience, for the next few years I tended to avoid Baptist churches. *No need to waste time there*, I thought.

Then something happened. In my neighborhood, I began to notice signs advertising a new Baptist church. They were holding services at a school just up the street from my house. Driving by their sign one Sunday, I made the decision to at least look into it. I would try one of their Bible studies.

---

[108] Jenkins, "Reconciling People."

The Bible study turned out to be relaxed, pleasant, and enlightening. The participants were of diverse racial and ethnic backgrounds and were obviously intelligent and well-educated. Best of all, the pastor was neither arrogant nor heavy-handed. I returned again on a number of occasions, and then decided to attend a Sunday service.

On my first Sunday attending the church, I found the hymns peaceful and uplifting. Each hymn had a depth of spiritual meaning, and the congregants sang harmoniously and from their hearts. The instrumental accompaniment was simple and muted, in contrast to the raucous blaring at some churches. This music was a balm to my soul. I felt at home. I felt God's presence in that place.

Toward the end of the service, it was time for communion. Unlike most of the other churches I had attended, this church did *not* welcome everyone to take communion. In fact, they cautioned against it.

The preacher strongly emphasized the importance of being worthy. He explained that if a person had sinned and had not yet repented, then he or she was not worthy and should let the bread and the cup pass. Furthermore, if one was not a Christian, then he or she was not worthy. Finally, although one may be a Christian, if one did not believe *exactly* as their church believed—based on the creed that we had just a moment ago recited—then that person should not partake of the communion.

Goodness! I was fully invested in this experience. I felt God's presence. I felt a love for these people and I respected them. That meant that I also had to respect their guidelines for participation. In their recitation of the creed, I knew that many of them were understanding resurrection in a physical sense, while I understood it in a spiritual sense. Thus, according to their understanding, I was not worthy.

As a hymn gently floated up from the piano and the communion trays made their way down row after row of seated congregants, I agonized.

Should I partake … or not?

I had shared the Eucharist at every other church.

What should I do?

I had to respect their wishes. I could not be a hypocrite and pretend to believe exactly as they did. Thus, in my heart I decided that I would have to pass the tray onward as it came down my row.

Then something happened.

My eyes were open, but as I sang the hymn I was turned inward toward God, experiencing the words of the hymn to the depths of my soul. And then, unexpectedly, *Jesus was there with me … at the very center of my being*. With his loving heart, he warmly embraced me and made it clear that *he* was inviting me to partake of the bread and wine.

Overwhelmed with gratitude for the love he was personally showing me, tears poured from my eyes and down my face. I could hardly breathe as I struggled not to sob aloud. When the communion tray came by, I gratefully took a cup and a tiny square of bread, held them for a moment, and gave thanks before I ate and drank.

I could not stop my tears. Even after I left the church, in my car, I was crying. People must have wondered about me, this guest.[109]

---

[109] I'm not unique among Unification Church members in having had personal experiences with Jesus. Testimonies abound from members who have had their own profound experience with him, sometimes on multiple occasions. My own remarkable encounter is a precious gift I will forever cherish.

True Father's Seonghwa

I had loved Jesus in my childhood, but my appreciation and love for him greatly deepened and expanded after I understood the *Divine Principle*. On top of that, Father Moon's sermons had the effect of enhancing and enriching a person's love for Jesus. In fact Father's discourses, especially in the earliest years of his ministry, were often about Jesus and, without fail, evoked the suffering heart of the Lord as, against all odds, he was trying to establish God's kingdom on earth, in his lifetime.

A reading of any one of Father's early sermons will demonstrate why his audiences were so often moved to tears. He was able to convey, as though he had been there himself, the intimate details and circumstances of Jesus's sad life.[110] No one who knows Reverend Moon can deny his remarkable love for—and unity with—the Lord.

---

[110] For example, see Sun Myung Moon, "The Incarnation of Jesus, A Pioneer," (February 1, 1959).

Part of the tragedy of Jesus's life was that although he came with the mission (as second Adam) of fulfilling the responsibility given to Adam and Eve (to become the perfect embodiments of God and the True Parents to all of humanity), Jesus was thwarted from doing so by the disbelief of the chosen people.

If Jesus in his lifetime had found faith on earth, if he had been accepted, then the Marriage of the Lamb[111] would have taken place at that time. There would have been no need for a Second Coming. Jesus and his Bride would have become our *True* Parents, replacing the *false* parents (the fallen Adam and Eve). And as our True Parents, they would have set the divine standard, modeling for *all* of humanity (male *and* female, parents and children) a life of absolute goodness.

In fact, the fulfillment of the divine will to establish True Parents on earth is the very reason that a Second Coming became necessary.

To remove any ambiguity for the reader, I believe that in unity with Jesus, Father and Mother Moon have completed the messianic mission of establishing the True Parents on earth. Because of this, humanity (which until now has been "of your father the devil," as Jesus made clear),[112] can now be restored to God's bosom by being engrafted as His children through receiving the blessing of marriage through the True Parents.

---

[111] *Revelation* 19:9 and 21: 9-10.
[112] *John* 8: 42-47.

On September 3, 2012, Father Moon ascended into the spiritual world. That event, although it had been preceded by a serious illness, seemed surreal. Our church family had not expected this day to come so soon, especially not just a few months short of the long-anticipated establishment of the Foundation Day of *Cheon Il Guk*,[113] which would commemorate a milestone in God's providence of salvation.

So many times throughout his life, True Father had surmounted impossible and even life-threatening conditions: imprisonment, torture, physical deprivation, and even that merciless, grueling personal schedule of his. That's why, although he was ninety-two years old, his ascension was so hard to believe. It seemed ironic and incomprehensible that he would succumb to an illness like pneumonia when he had survived so much worse. Of course, few of us back then were aware that his lungs had been damaged when, as a young man, he had dug, bagged, and hauled nitrogen fertilizer at the Hungnam prison labor camp. In the end, his body had simply reached the limits of endurance.

---

[113] *Cheon Il Guk* can be translated from the Korean as "Nation of Cosmic Peace and Unity." These words express God's hope for a global nation encompassing all of humanity living together in peace.

Although I had never traveled to Korea before then, I felt a personal sense of urgency about going there to attend Father's *seonghwa*.[114]

In all my years as a Unificationist, when we had commemorated the lives of people who had passed on, we were educated—and even exhorted—to keep a joyful and uplifted mind. This was, in part, to celebrate and encourage the person who was transitioning to his or her eternal life. As recently as May 2011, Father and Mother had shared about this topic:

> Ladies and gentlemen, the word death is sacred. It is not a noun of sadness and suffering. True Parents have created the term Seonghwa [ascension] to explain the true significance of death. The moment we enter the spirit world should be a time that we enter a world of joy and victory with the fruits born of our lives on earth. It is a time for those of us remaining on earth to send off the departed with joy. It should be a time for great celebration. That is the way of the sacred and noble Seonghwa Ceremony, the first step the spirit of the departed takes toward enjoying eternal life in attendance to God, within His embrace.[115]

As much as I meditated on this as I made my way to Korea, I could not find within myself that spirit of celebration

---

[114] In the Unification tradition, a *seonghwa* ceremony is the commemoration and celebration of a person's life after he or she ascends.

[115] S.M. Moon and H.J.H. Moon, "Settlement of True Parents," 247-8.

or of victorious departure. All I felt was an overwhelming sense of grief. I could not imagine life without True Father on earth. As I thought of others who were on their way to Korea, I wondered: Will *they* be joyful and uplifted? Will this seonghwa be a celebration of Father's life?

When I arrived in Korea, there was nowhere even a pretense of being joyful. The hearts of the people around me were broken. At the seonghwa ceremony itself, although True Mother held her grieving in check, it was clearly overwhelming and palpable. I had never before seen Mother like this.

And yet, as I anticipated the eulogies and the testimonies, I still hoped there would be indications that we should encourage and uplift our Father as he began his eternal life in the spiritual world. I looked for consolation, perhaps a statement of divine purpose, a good reason for Heaven to have called Father away at this particular time.

In his eulogy, Hyung Jin Moon, one of the sons of the True Parents, alluded to such a divine purpose. He said,

> True Father had the task of opening the gates of heaven prior to Foundation Day for the myriads of people in the spirit world. Cheon Il Guk cannot be a kingdom only for those on earth. If Cheon Il Guk is on earth, it must also exist in the heavenly world, and if Cheon Il Guk exists in the heavenly world, it must also exist on earth. Consequently, with 172 days remaining until … Foundation Day, True Father went to the heavenly world while entrusting this final task on earth to True Mother and to all blessed family members….

> Therefore, on the 13th day of the 1st month of the heavenly calendar in 2013, True Mother on earth, and True Father in heaven shall simultaneously proclaim the Foundation Day of Cheon Il Guk.[116]

On the following day, True Mother said something similar.

> True Father's seonghwa brings me, after being together with him my whole life, unfathomable pain and sorrow. It is the same for all of you. Moreover, we cannot begin to fathom the sorrowful heart of God, who is the original substance of eternal love and the True Parent of humankind.
>
> From another aspect, this is also a time of hope. True Father worked in accordance with the heavenly laws— which God established at the time of the creation of heaven and earth—to conclude, complete and perfect all the providential tasks on earth that no one in human history had been able to fulfill. He is now transitioning to the spirit world to exercise dominion over both the spiritual and physical worlds and initiate a new dimension of God's providence. No spoken or written language … can possibly express the flood of emotions we experience as we stand at this juncture in the providence.[117]

As I sat there looking down from an upper tier of the 25,000-seat auditorium of the Cheong Shim Peace World Center, I felt the crushed hearts of the worldwide family gathered there. We were struggling mightily to contain our grief.

---

[116] H.J. Moon, "Seonghwa Address."
[117] H.J.H. Moon, "Let Us Inherit."

It was very likely Dr. Bo Hi Pak's prayer, honest words from the heart of a close disciple, that precipitated the bursting of the dam of pent-up grief and allowed a deluge of sorrow to sweep through the auditorium. He prayed,

Heavenly Father!

How come you so hurriedly called True Father to your side? What about us, your poor children who still need him? It feels like the heavens are falling and the ground is giving way underneath us. Our surroundings have become a dark heaven and earth, as though the sun has lost its light. We attended True Father as though he was our life and sun, and now that he is gone, sadness endlessly overflows from our hearts....[118]

Dr. Pak's thoughts were our thoughts. His personal sense of loss and confusion was ours as well. It must have been at this point in his prayer that the floodwaters found a crack and the dam broke. From a section of the stadium to my left, a few stifled sobs escaped and reverberated in the stillness. Then, like a tsunami, a general weeping arose, intensifying and surging forward, traveling around the stadium.

When the wave of spilled-over grief reached me, it crashed and broke, and my own sobs merged with the flood, which continued to sweep around the stadium. I buried my face and tried not to breathe because to breathe was to weep, and to weep was to wail. That wave of uncontrollable grief

---

[118] Pak, "Prayer."

surged and undulated around the stadium until it had engulfed the entire body of congregants.

All the while Dr. Pak, himself choking on his tears, continued with his prayer.

Heavenly Father,

It is *true* that we have not been filial. When True Father was sleeping for only two hours a day, not hesitating to go to distant places, constantly going back and forth, even though we saw True Father working so hard, we did not pay attention to his suffering. Please forgive the immaturity of your poor children.

Dearest True Father!

…. We wish we could hear your voice just one more time…. While you loved the members, while you loved humanity, you completely forgot about yourself. You never took care of yourself, overworking yourself again and again. Is there a single moment when you ever truly rested? [119]

On the day following Father's seonghwa, despite her own grief Mother Moon stepped forward to comfort, encourage, and uplift the worldwide membership. She assured us that her unity with Father and his continuing participation from heaven would ensure the continuity and completion of the messianic mission. We would move forward to substantiate the kingdom of God on earth, a world of lasting peace, harmony, abundance, and joy, in loving union with God.

---

[119] Pak, "Prayer."

Mother of Peace

Who is Mother Moon? As the new Eve, as God's begotten daughter, she has been sent to fulfill—along with the returning Adam—the role of True Parents. As already explained, True Parents are indispensable for engrafting fallen humanity back into God's lineage and for guiding us to recover our status as God's children. In this way the ideal of creation, the original hope and plan of our Heavenly Parent, will be fulfilled.

Looking back now, I see that as a young member I mistook True Mother's quiet support for her husband as evidence of feminine subordination. I failed to notice that it was *together* that they carried the messianic burdens. Together they made personal sacrifices, labored without rest, and traveled back and forth across the globe in service to humanity. And when at last, aged and exhausted, Father could no longer take another step, when he passed over into the world of eternal life, Mother picked up the cross and continued walking.

I see True Mother's function as being that of the Holy Spirit manifested on earth. In her I see the value of a woman who reflects the divine feminine, the motherly aspect of God.

To some, the concept of the feminine aspect of God— or of God as our Heavenly Mother—might seem as radical as when Jesus first proclaimed that God was "our Father" and that "he who has seen me has seen the Father."[120] But for me, Mother Moon embodies what it means to exist as a woman "in the image and likeness" of God who is the "Heavenly *Parent*, the harmonious, perfected union of Heavenly Father and Heavenly Mother."[121]

Mother Moon is God's daughter. She exemplifies the divine heart, which guides humanity with empathy and compassion. She gives of herself, nurtures, and uplifts. Her life demonstrates the truth that women, who are created to reflect and represent the feminine aspect of God, are irreplaceable partners in the family, in society, and in the world. Such are the qualities of the selfless love I see in Mother Moon.

Based on my observations, Mother appears to have stepped up as a public figure gradually. I noticed the beginnings of it in 1984 when Father was unjustly sent to

---

[120] *John* 14: 9.
[121] Hak Ja Han Moon, *Mother of Peace*, 329. Emphasis added.

Danbury Prison and Mother assumed greater responsibility for leading the movement.[122]

Later, she became a champion for women and a prominent peacemaker in her own right. In September 1991, she addressed the Tokyo convention of the Women's Federation for World Peace in Asia. Then in 1992, the global era of women having arrived, Mother ascended to the world stage as the True Mother and as God's daughter.[123] In April of that year, she inaugurated the Women's Federation for World Peace (WFWP) and called on women around the globe to serve as mediators of peace and forgiveness.[124] In December, she spoke in the Great Hall of the People in Tiananmen Square. Even in China, she dared to speak about God.[125] By the year 2000, True Mother had spoken publicly in six hundred locations around the world.[126]

A woman of vision, True Mother views her role in this way:

> To fulfill my mission as God's only begotten Daughter, I have a firm belief and unflinching will for the sake of every nation, every religion, every race. Going beyond all fallen world boundaries, I am called to reconcile

---

[122] For a detailed account of the period, see H.J.H. Moon, *Mother of Peace*, 149-158.

[123] Sunhak Institute of History, *True Mother … Anthology*, 128-129.

[124] Sunhak, 128-9.

[125] H.J.H. Moon, *Mother of Peace*, 162-163.

[126] Sunhak, *True Mother* 129.

nations and races with benevolence and love. I am called to be like the ocean that accepts and absorbs the water of all rivers, big and small alike. Embodying our God who is our Heavenly Mother as well as (our) Heavenly Father, I am called to embrace all who are lost and have no one to receive them, with the heart of a parent."[127]

Among other responsibilities, True Mother officiates at Holy Marriage Blessings as she uplifts godly families, which are the foundation of a peaceful world.[128] She sustains the humanitarian and peace-building organizations that she and Father Moon founded together, and creates new coalitions that promote peace. Organizations like the Universal Peace Federation (UPF) and the International Association of Parliamentarians for Peace (IAPP) bring together leaders of nations and world religions in search of common ground and peaceful ways of reconciling differences.

Fulfilling the divine plan involves healing the human interactions within and among families, societies, and nations.[129] But it also requires facilitating the realization of God's third blessing, as expressed in *Genesis* 1:26 and 28, that humanity assume the responsibility of being stewards of the

[127] H.J.H. Moon, *Mother of Peace*, 93.

[128] For information on how to receive the Holy Marriage Blessing, contact your local Unification Church, the Family Federation for World Peace and Unification, or the author at piloteeby@gmail.com.

[129] In this way, the first two blessings or divine imperatives to "be fruitful" (i.e. mature or perfect) "and multiply" are realized. *Genesis* 1:28

planet. To that end, Mother Moon promotes environmental consciousness and stewardship through associations and organizations like the Sunhak Peace Prize and the Hyo Jeong International Foundation for the Unity of the Sciences.

Finally—but first and foremost in importance—as she reaches out to the world to bring healing and peace, True Mother reminds us that lasting peace requires placing God, our Heavenly Parent, at the center of our existence. These are just some of the reasons why people around the globe are coming to recognize Mother Moon as God's Only Begotten Daughter, the Mother of Peace.[130]

---

[130] https://motherofpeace.com/.

Blessed are the Peacemakers

I am grateful that over the years I have been able to support—even to a small extent—these peace-building endeavors. But what difference does one individual make? The answer is: all the difference in the world.

I may be a speck in the cosmos, an infinitesimal fraction of the whole, but I know that each and every human being—without exception—is of infinite value to the Creator. Made "in His image and likeness," every one of us is unique and irreplaceable. Because we each reflect various aspects of God, our contributions to the universe are essential. The unique qualities, gifts, or talents that each person has are what make the world a joyful and hospitable place. Thus, to our Heavenly Parent—and ideally to one another—every person is infinitely precious.

I am grateful for having walked this path. Discovering the *Divine Principle* has pointed me in the direction of developing a direct relationship with God, of living with God at the core of my being and at the center of my life. Because of this I can be at peace regardless of external circumstances.

Informed by the *Principle*, I can distinguish good from evil and make wiser choices. I am relieved of the burdens of resentment and hostility because I am able to forgive those who do harm … because I know that they do so out of ignorance.

I'm grateful for God's choice of my husband and for the holy marriage blessing that gave us three wonderful children and many beautiful and amazing grandchildren. For the unified global family of which I am a part, each member of which strives to live in ways worthy of being a child of God, I am grateful.

Finally, I thank God for having blessed me, in my childhood, with that life-changing night vision and for having guided my way, in spite of my decade-long "amnesia" and a temporary loss of faith, to the eventual fulfillment of that revelation. In other words, I am grateful for having traveled the journey that began with the angel, the book, and the secret.

Works Cited

"April Blows in Like March" and "Rev. Moon Goes on Trial in City on Tax Charges." *New York Times,* April 2, 1982, B2.

"Blessing Ceremony of the Unification Church," https://en.wikipedia.org/wiki/Blessing_ceremony_of_the_Unification_Church#cite_ref-14. Accessed September 14, 2020.

Breen, Michael. *Sun Myung Moon: the early years 1920-53.* West Sussex, U.K. Refuge Books, 1997.

"Communion Hymn," anonymous. https://www.youtube.com/watch?v=4tkcFDNcRaY. Accessed December 29, 2020.

Curry, George E. "Clerics Urge Pardon for Reverend Moon." Chicago Tribune. https://www.chicagotribune.com/news/ct-xpm-1985-08-21-8502240616-story.html. Accessed December 30, 2020.

Dadachanji, Dinshaw, ed. 2020. *Resolving Environmental Threats for the Benefit of Humanity: Proceedings of the Twenty-Sixth International Conference on the Unity of the Sciences,*

Washington, DC: Hyo Jeong International Foundation for the Unity of the Sciences Press.

Devine, Tony. "The First National Divine Principle Workshop in the Soviet Union." In *40 Years in America: An Intimate History of the Unification Movement 1959-1999*, edited by Michael Inglis, pp. 357-361. New York, NY. HSA Publications, 2000.

Dubisz, Claus. "The Fourth CARP Convention of World Students." http://www.tparents.org/Moon-Talks/hyojinmoon/HyoJinMoon-870808.htm. Accessed August 31, 2020.

"Fall of the Berlin Wall." https://en.wikipedia.org/wiki/Fall_of_the_Berlin_Wall. Accessed August 31, 2020.

Family Federation for World Peace and Unification. http://familyfed.org/ Accessed December 29, 2020.

"Family Pledge." Family Federation for World Peace and Unification. https://www.ffwpu.asn.au/1%20Family%20Pledge.pdf

Friend, Theodore P. "Moon's Financial Rise and Fall." https://www.thecrimson.com/article/1984/10/11/moons-financial-rise-and-fall-pbab/#:~:text=Sixteen%20amicus%20briefs%20representing%2043,trial%20and%20the%20subsequent%20appeals. Accessed March 24, 2022.

Hatch, Orrin. Letter to Mr. Edward Bennett Williams, quoted by Paul Cobb, "Moon Victim of Gov't Conspiracy," *The Los Angeles Times*, July 15, 1985, p. 11. https://www.newspapers.com/newspage/401468773/ . Accessed February 27, 2021.

"Issues in Religious Liberty." Hearing Before the Subcommittee on the Constitution of the Committee on the Judiciary. United States Senate, Ninety-Eighth Congress, Second Session on Oversight on the State of Religious Liberty in America Today, June 26, 1984. Serial No. J-98-124. U.S. Government Printing Office. Washington, DC. 1985 https://files.eric.ed.gov/fulltext/ED257762.pdf. Accessed February 25, 2021.

Jenkins, Michael W. "Reconciling People of the Abrahamic Faiths." Universal Peace Federation. https://www.upf.org/peace-and-security/middle-east-peace-programs/1679-reconciling-the-abrahamic-faiths. Accessed December 31, 2020.

Jones, Farley. *A Heart Made Whole: My Spiritual Journey.* Middletown, DE. February 01, 2020.

Joo, Douglas, ed. 2020. "Preface." In *Exploring New Pathways to Resolve Environmental Challenges: Proceedings of the First International Conference on Science and God*, Washington, DC: Hyo Jeong International Foundation for the Unity of the Sciences Press.

Khachigian, Kenneth L. "Renaming John Wayne Airport Would Tarnish One More Idol: Democrats Should Take a Second Look at FDR and Others Before Opening that Door." *The Washington Times.* Online edition 7/9/2020, page B 03. https://www.washingtontimes.com/news/2020/jul/8/renaming-john-wayne-airport-would-tarnish-one-more/. Accessed January 24, 2021.

"Koreagate," https://en.wikipedia.org/wiki/Koreagate. Accessed December 29, 2020.

Kwak, Chung Hwan; Stadler, Christa Segato; Grabner, Barbara, editors. *Mission Butterfly: Pioneers Behind the Iron Curtain.* Bratislava, Slovakia. Family Federation for World Peace, 2006.

Lamoreaux, J.W., Flake, L. The Russian Orthodox Church, the Kremlin, and religious (il)liberalism in Russia. Palgrave Commun 4, 115 (2018). https://doi.org/10.1057/s41599-018-0169-6 or https://www.nature.com/articles/s41599-018-0169-6 Accessed March 6, 2022.

Lee, Sang Hun. *Communism: A Critique and Counterproposal.* Washington, D.C. The Freedom Leadership Foundation, Inc. 1973.

Mickler, Michael. "Educating Soviet Leaders and Youth." In *40 Years in America: An Intimate History of the Unification Movement 1959-1999*, edited by Michael Inglis, pp. 353-356. New York, NY. HSA Publications, 2000.

Moon, Hak Ja Han. "Let Us Inherit the Realm of True
    Parents' Victory and Open a Future Filled with Hope."
    truelove.org/HJHSpeeches/2012/HakJaHan-
    120916.pdf. Accessed February 27, 2020.

---. *Mother of Peace: A Memoir*. English edition. Washington,
    D.C.: The Washington Times Global Media Group,
    2020.

---. "True Mother's Message on 60th Anniversary of True
    Parents' Holy Wedding."
    http://familyfedihq.org/2020/05/true-mothers-
    message-on-60th-anniversary-of-true-parents-holy-
    wedding/. Accessed June 30, 2020.

Moon, Hyung Jin. "Seonghwa Address."
    www.tparents.org/moon-talks/HyungJinMoon-
    12/HyungJinMoon-120915.htm. Accessed February
    27, 2020.

Moon, Sun Myung. *As a Peace-Loving Global Citizen*. The
    Washington Times Foundation, 2009. Online text
    available at: https://www.tparents.org/Moon-
    Books/PLGC-SunMyungMoon-091101.pdf. Accessed
    October 5, 2021.

---. *Exposition of the Divine Principle*. New York: The Holy
    Spirit Association for the Unification of World
    Christianity. Second edition, 2006.
    www.tparents.org/Library/Unification/Books/DP06/
    0-Toc.htm. Accessed February 27, 2020.

---. "The God of Heart." In *Cheon Seong Gyeong: An Anthology of True Parents' Teachings,* edited by the Committee for the Compilation of True Parents' Words, 53. Korea: Family Federation for World Peace and Unification, Seonghwa Publications, English edition, 2014.

---. "The Incarnation of Jesus, A Pioneer." https://www.tparents.org/Moon-Talks/SunMyungMoon59/SunMyungMoon-590201.htm. Accessed February 4, 2023.

---. "The Path of Humanity and the United States in the Era of the Peace Kingdom." In *Pyeong Hwa Gyeong: The Holy Scripture of Cheon Il Guk,* edited by the Committee for the Compilation of True Parents' Words, 1436-1448. Seoul, Korea: Family Federation for World Peace and Unification, Seonghwa Publications. English edition, 2014.

---. "Realization of a Peaceful World through the Ideal of True Families." In *Pyeong Hwa Gyeong: The Holy Scripture of Cheon Il Guk,* edited by the Committee for the Compilation of True Parents' Words, 558. Seoul, Korea: Family Federation for World Peace and Unification, Seonghwa Publications. English edition, 2014.

Moon, Sun Myung and Moon, Hak Ja Han. "The Settlement of the True Parents of Heaven, Earth and Humankind Who, as God's Embodiment, Proclaim the Word." *True Mother Hak Ja Han Moon: An Anthology III:*

Cheon Il Guk and Our Mission, edited by Sunhak Institute of History, Seoul: Sung Hwa Publishing, Inc., 2018, 242-261.

Mother of Peace (website). https://motherofpeace.com/.

Nadeau, Jean-Francois, "Quand le KKK faisait sa loi contre les Canadiens francais du Maine." In *Le Devoir*, June 8, 2021. https://www.ledevoir.com/societe/608667/histoire-quand-le-kkk-faisait-sa-loi-contre-les-canadiens-francais-du-maine?fbclid=IwAR2osNZY394GTeNnSJDZx-F7FOaL8kz6G1LRR3lEkKQjtOUHYMvhx80uH2k. Accessed September 4, 2021.

"New Era Ecumenical Conferences." Tparents.org. https://www.tparents.org/Library/Unification/Books/40Years/40-4-22a.htm

"Nicene Creed." https://www3.nd.edu/~afreddos/courses/43801/creeds.pdf. Accessed July 3, 2020.

Pak, Bo Hi. "Prayer at Sun Myung Moon's Seunghwa." www.tparents.org/Moon-Talks/SunMyungMoon12/SunMyungMoon-120915.pdf. Accessed February 27, 2020.

"Peace Starts with Me." https://peacestartswithme.lpages.co/virtual-rally/. Accessed December 29, 2020.

Peemoeller, Gerhard. *Bodyguard for Christ.* Self-published, 2010.

Professors World Peace Academy. Second International Congress, "The Fall of the Soviet Empire: Prospects for Transition to a Post-Soviet World." https://www.pwpa.org/second-international-congress-the-fall-of-the-soviet-empire-prospects-for-transition-to-a-post-soviet-world/

"Rally of Hope," https://www.rallyofhope.org/. Accessed January 24, 2021.

Seuk, Joon Ho. "The Soviet Student International Leadership Conference (ILC)." http://www.tparents.org/Library/Unification/Talks2/Seuk/Seuk-901000.htm. Accessed December 31, 2020.

"Statement of Purpose," ACLC. https://www.aclcnational.org/category/who-we-are/. Accessed September 17, 2020.

Sunhak Institute of History, editor. *True Mother Hak Ja Han Moon: An Anthology IV: True Mother in the Eyes of True Father: May You Blossom, My Beloved.* Seoul: Sung Hwa Publishing, Inc. 2018.

"True Mother at the Africa Summit." http://familyfedihq.org/2018/01/true-mother-at-the-africa-summit/ Accessed December 29, 2020.

"True Mother's World Tour Schedule." http://www.tparents.org/Moon-Talks/HakJaHan-

19/HakJaHan-190831.pdf. Accessed December 29, 2020.

United States v. Moon, 718 F. 2d 1210 (2nd Cir., 1983).

"United States v. Sun Myung Moon." *Wikipedia.* https://en.wikipedia.org/wiki/United_States_v._Sun_Myung_Moon. Accessed September 1, 2020.

"United States v. Sun Myung Moon." *Wikipedia.* https://en.wikipedia.org/wiki/United_States_v._Sun_Myung_Moon#Commentary_and_protests : Accessed March 24, 2022.

Universal Peace Federation. https://www.upf.org/. Accessed January 24, 2021.

"What are the answers to the Four Questions?" Chabad.org. https://www.chabad.org/holidays/passover/pesach_cdo/aid/511100/jewish/Answers-to-the-4-Questions.htm. Accessed July 23, 2020.

Wilson, Andrew, ed. *World Scripture: A Comparative Anthology of Sacred Texts*. International Religious Foundation, 1991. https://www.unification.net/ws/ Accessed December 29, 2020.

Acknowledgments

First and foremost, I am thankful for the unconditional love of God, our Heavenly Parent, who guides and protects us over the course of our life journeys.

For their patience and forbearance, along the way of my writing this memoir, I thank my entire family. Though we differ in outlook regarding some of the issues touched upon in the book, I am grateful to Carl Cicone, Christopher Eby, Stephanie Eby, William Pilote, and Louise Tancrede for their investment of time and for sharing with me their honest perspectives and suggestions regarding the text.

I'm equally grateful to every friend who weighed in with an opinion or fact check. Thank you, Reginald Audrick, Ora Cooke, Lynn Criner, Dan Fefferman, Peter Gogan, Dominique Johnston, David Kasbow, Nicholas Kernan, Vicki Phelps, Richard Steinbronn, Cheryl Wetzstein, Rhonda Williams, and John Willis for your helpful insights, corrections, suggestions, and words of encouragement, all of which mean so much to me.

There will forever be a special place in my heart for the "Writing Sibs" Nancy Bulow, Susan Fefferman, Steven

Matthew Goldberg, Libby Jo Henkin, Mary Johnson, Larry Moffitt, and Pamela Stein, all of whom have contributed to my development as a writer and who have offered helpful feedback on various portions of the text. I owe a special debt of gratitude to Pamela, not only for her initiative—like a hand reaching down from heaven—at assembling our little group, but also for her ongoing support, which has been invaluable to me.

Finally—although first in terms of making a vital first impression—I'm grateful for the expert and tasteful design of the book's cover. Many thanks to you, Angela Eisenbart!

Thank You for Reading

If you found this book at all worthwhile or engaging, then please consider leaving an honest review on my Amazon or Barnes and Noble book pages. I greatly value your feedback and comments!
https://www.amazon.com/dp/B0CL2VPQ4Y/ and https://www.barnesandnoble.com/w/book/1144225161.

Growing up in the French-Canadian community of Lewiston, Maine, I first began examining issues of faith and doctrine as a Roman Catholic and, later, as a non-sectarian seeker. As a college student at Brandeis University, still unable to find satisfactory answers to my theological questions, I eventually resigned myself to agnosticism, and then to atheism.

Only when I encountered the teachings of the *Divine Principle* was I able to experience the reality of God in the cosmos and within human existence. That is why, for the past fifty years, I have been a member of the Unification movement.

As you can imagine, I enjoy pondering and discussing issues of spirituality and theology. It was as an avid student of religion that I earned a Master of Divinity degree from Union Theological Seminary. My interest in

Slavic studies also led me to pursue Master of Arts and Master of Philosophy degrees in Russian literature from Columbia University.

Now I'm in Maryland, a retired educator, mother, and grandmother with family ties that stretch north-south from Maine to Ecuador and westward to Colorado.

Again, thank you for reading! Feel free to send me inquiries or to chat at piloteeby@gmail.com.